1001
AMAZING SCIENCE FACTS

All rights are reserved 2024 by Life Style Daily. No part of this publication may be reproduced, stored in a retrieval system or transmitted in any form or by any means, electronic, mechanical, photocopying, recording or otherwise, without prior permission.

Table of Contents

Chapter 1: Mysteries of the Universe 6

    1. The Formation of Stars 6

    2. Black Holes and Their Power 7

    3. Exoplanets 9

    4. Life on Other Planets – Facts and Speculations 10

Chapter 2: The Astonishing Properties of Earth 14

    1. Earth's Atmosphere and Its Wonders 14

    2. Incredible Geological Phenomena 15

    3. Extreme Places on Earth 17

    4. Water – The Source of Life 18

    5. Evolution and Climate Change 20

Chapter 3: Biological Phenomena 22

    1. Genetics – The Code of Life 22

    2. Fascinating Animal Abilities 23

    3. Plants That Amaze 25

    4. Microorganisms – Invisible Wonders 26

    5. The Human Body by the Numbers 28

Chapter 4: Amazing Scientific Discoveries 29

    1. Epoch-Making Inventions 29

    2. The Most Surprising Experiments 31

    3. Brilliant Mistakes That Changed the World 33

    4. Unresolved Mysteries of Science 34

    5. Technologies of the Future 36

Chapter 5: Wonders of Physics 38
1. Quantum Oddities 38
2. Relativity in Practice 39
3. Sound and Waves – The Invisible Power 41
4. Light and Optics 42
5. Magnetic and Electrical Phenomena 44

Chapter 6: Chemistry in Everyday Life 46
1. Fascinating Properties of Elements 46
2. Chemical Reactions in the Kitchen 47
3. Substances That Changed the World 49
4. Toxicity and Antidotes 50
5. Surprising Facts About Polymers and Plastics 52

Chapter 7: Time and Space 54
1. The History of Time and the Calendar 54
2. Dimensions and Their Interpretation 55
3. Time Travel – Science or Fiction? 57
4. Gravity and Its Mysteries 58
5. Planetary Motion and Cosmic Harmony 60

Chapter 8: Mysteries of the Human Mind 62
1. How Does the Brain Work? 62
2. Senses – Our Tools of Perception 63
3. Dreams and Their Significance 65
4. Neurobiology of Emotions 66
5. Cognitive Abilities and Their Limits 68

Chapter 9: Evolution and the History of Life 70

    1. The Origins of Life on Earth 70

    2. Dinosaurs – Facts That Amaze 71

    3. Mass Extinctions in Planetary History 73

    4. The Evolution of Humans 75

    5. The Genome and Its Mysteries 76

Chapter 10. Unsolved Mysteries of Science 79

    1. Mysterious Natural Phenomena 79

    2. Do Other Universes Exist? 80

    3. Dark Energy and Dark Matter 82

    4. Extraterrestrial Intelligence – Evidence and Hypotheses 83

    5. Future of Science – Unanswered Questions 85

    6. Barriers and Breakthroughs in Science 87

An Ode to Curiosity and the Power of Science 89

In a world full of mysteries, science stands as our most powerful tool for uncovering, understanding, and shaping reality. For centuries, it has enabled us to push the boundaries of imagination, explain phenomena once deemed magical, and open doors to endless possibilities. Through science, we have learned to gaze at the stars, examine the smallest elements of matter, and delve into the profound mysteries of the human mind.

This book invites you on a journey through the most fascinating realms of knowledge – from the origins of life on Earth to the vast complexity of the cosmos and the groundbreaking discoveries that have reshaped our world. But it is not just a collection of facts and theories; it also explores the questions that remain unanswered: What is consciousness? Do other universes exist? What limits remain for humanity to overcome?

The purpose of this book is not only to share knowledge but also to ignite curiosity – the foundation of every discovery. In a world where technology and science advance faster than ever before, it becomes increasingly evident that the questions we ask drive progress. This relentless quest to understand the universe, from the tiniest particles to its grandest structures, defines us as a species of explorers.

As you turn the pages of this book, I invite you to reflect on the past, present, and future of science. Each chapter is a tribute to human curiosity and perseverance – qualities that inspire us to dream of the impossible and turn those dreams into reality. Perhaps this journey will encourage you to view the world around us from a new perspective, to ask fresh questions, and to seek your own answers.

After all, the beauty of science lies in its ability to continuously surprise and inspire us.

Chapter 1: Mysteries of the Universe

1. The Formation of Stars

1. Stars are born in immense clouds of gas and cosmic dust called nebulae.

2. The process of star formation begins when gravity concentrates mass in one area, creating a dense protostar.

3. The most famous "stellar nursery" is the Orion Nebula, visible to the naked eye from Earth.

4. Massive stars form faster than smaller ones, sometimes within millions of years, while smaller stars may take billions of years.

5. Newly formed stars emit powerful stellar winds that clear the surrounding area of gas and dust.

6. Only 1% of the material in a nebula turns into stars, while the rest becomes planets, asteroids, or is expelled into space.

7. Stars form in groups called clusters and are often born alongside hundreds of others.

8. A star's core ignites when the temperature reaches around 10 million degrees Kelvin, initiating nuclear fusion.

9. Nuclear fusion in young stars fuses hydrogen atoms into helium, releasing vast amounts of energy.

10. Stars with greater mass burn fuel faster than smaller ones, meaning their lifespans are shorter.

11. The smallest stars, known as red dwarfs, can live for trillions of years.

12. Massive stars may end their lives as supernovae, while smaller stars become white dwarfs.

13. The Crab Nebula, visible in the sky, is the remnant of a supernova explosion observed in 1054 AD.

14. The oldest known stars are over 13 billion years old, nearly as ancient as the universe itself.

15. Stars appear in different colors based on their temperature – the hottest are blue, while the coolest are red.

16. Most of the stars we see at night are part of our galaxy, the Milky Way.

17. Stars undergo life cycles – from their birth in nebulae to their deaths as black holes, neutron stars, or white dwarfs.

18. On average, about seven new stars are born each year in our galaxy.

19. The largest known stars, like Betelgeuse, have diameters hundreds of times greater than that of the Sun.

20. Star formation in massive molecular clouds is observed using X-ray and radio telescopes.

2. Black Holes and Their Power

21. Black holes are formed when massive stars end their lives through gravitational collapse.

22. The gravity of a black hole is so strong that nothing, not even light, can escape from it.

23. The event horizon is the boundary around a black hole beyond which nothing can escape.

24. Supermassive black holes are located at the centers of most galaxies, including the Milky Way.

25. Black holes can grow in mass by "devouring" matter, gas, and other stars that come near them.

26. The largest known black holes have masses billions of times greater than the mass of the Sun.

27. Black holes can merge with one another, creating even more massive objects through collisions.

28. The discovery of gravitational waves in 2015 confirmed black hole collisions, as predicted by Einstein's theory.

29. Miniature black holes, known as primordial black holes, may have masses smaller than stars, though their existence is not yet confirmed.

30. X-rays and radio emissions help scientists detect black holes, even though they are invisible to optical telescopes.

31. The process of "spaghettification" describes what happens to objects pulled into black holes – they are stretched lengthwise by extreme gravitational forces.

32. Stephen Hawking demonstrated that black holes can "evaporate" through the emission of Hawking radiation, leading to their gradual disappearance.

33. Black holes can form accretion disks – hot, spinning rings of gas and matter around the event horizon.

34. Sagittarius A* is the supermassive black hole at the center of the Milky Way, located about 27,000 light-years from Earth.

35. Black holes play a crucial role in shaping galaxy evolution, influencing their structure and star formation.

36. In 2019, the first photograph of a black hole in the galaxy M87 was captured through the Event Horizon Telescope collaboration.

37. The gravity of black holes can warp spacetime, causing effects like time dilation – time moves more slowly near them.

38. Black holes do not "swallow" everything in their vicinity – objects must cross the event horizon to be pulled in.

39. Streams of matter, called relativistic jets, can be ejected from the areas surrounding black holes, despite their immense gravitational pull.

40. Observing black holes allows scientists to test Einstein's theory of relativity under extreme conditions.

3. Exoplanets

41. Exoplanets, also known as extrasolar planets, are planets orbiting stars other than the Sun.

42. The first exoplanet was discovered in 1992, orbiting the pulsar PSR B1257+12.

43. In 1995, the first exoplanet orbiting a Sun-like star, 51 Pegasi b, was discovered.

44. To date, the existence of over 5,000 exoplanets has been confirmed in various star systems.

45. Exoplanets are primarily detected using two methods: the transit method (changes in a star's brightness) and the radial velocity method (gravitational effects on a star).

46. Planets can exist in the so-called habitable zone, where temperatures allow for liquid water.

47. Exoplanets are highly diverse – from hot Jupiters to super-Earths and icy worlds.

48. Hot Jupiters are gas giants that orbit very close to their stars, resulting in extremely high temperatures.

49. Super-Earths are exoplanets with a mass greater than Earth but less than Neptune.

50. Kepler-22b is one of the first exoplanets discovered in the habitable zone of its star.

51. The exoplanet HD 189733 b has an atmosphere with glass-like rain falling horizontally at speeds of 8,700 km/h (5,400 mph).

52. Water, methane, carbon dioxide, and other chemical compounds detected in exoplanet atmospheres may indicate the potential for life.

53. The planet WASP-12b is so close to its star that it is gradually being "consumed" by the star's gravity.

54. Exoplanets can have moons, but no exomoon has yet been directly confirmed.

55. The TRAPPIST-1 system contains seven Earth-sized planets, three of which are in the habitable zone.

56. Some exoplanets may be rogue objects drifting in interstellar space, not bound to any star.

57. Detection methods for exoplanets are becoming increasingly advanced, with new missions like the TESS telescope and the James Webb Space Telescope aiding in discoveries.

58. Exoplanets reflecting their star's light can be studied using spectroscopy, allowing for the analysis of their atmospheres.

59. Earth is the only known planet with life, but discovering exoplanets raises hopes of finding life beyond the Solar System.

60. Future space missions could send probes to nearby exoplanets, such as Proxima Centauri b, to study them directly.

4. Life on Other Planets – Facts and Speculations

61. Earth is the only known planet with life, but scientists are constantly searching for signs of it beyond the Solar System.

62. Mars is a primary target for the search for life in the Solar System, as evidence suggests liquid water existed there in the past.

63. Europa, a moon of Jupiter, may harbor an ocean beneath its icy crust, making it one of the most promising places to search for life.

64. Enceladus, a moon of Saturn, emits water plumes containing organic particles, suggesting potential conditions for life.

65. Titan, Saturn's largest moon, has hydrocarbon lakes and an atmosphere rich in methane, which could provide an alternative environment for life.

66. Proxima Centauri b, an exoplanet in the habitable zone of the closest star to the Sun, is a key candidate for the search for life.

67. Scientists study so-called biosignatures – chemical traces of life, such as oxygen, methane, or ozone, in exoplanet atmospheres.

68. In 2020, phosphine was detected in the atmosphere of Venus, sparking speculation about the possibility of microorganisms in its clouds.

69. Many microorganisms on Earth, known as extremophiles, can survive in extreme conditions, suggesting life might exist on other planets.

70. There are theories that life on Earth may have arrived from space via meteorites – a concept known as panspermia.

71. Space missions, such as the James Webb Space Telescope, enable the study of exoplanet atmospheres in the search for potential signs of life.

72. The discovery of liquid water on Mars has raised hopes of finding microorganisms in its soil.

73. In 1976, the Viking probes conducted the first experiments on Mars to detect life, but the results were inconclusive.

74. The "dark biosphere" hypothesis suggests that life might exist in forms completely different from those known on Earth.

75. Sun-like stars with planets in the habitable zone are a priority in the search for life in the galaxy.

76. Life could exist beneath the surface of planets like Mars or Europa, where it would be shielded from radiation.

77. Some exoplanets may have oceans similar to Earth's, making them potentially hospitable to life.

78. Speculations about alien civilizations, such as the SETI project, focus on searching for radio signals from space.

79. Fermi's Paradox questions why, if the universe is abundant with life, we have yet to detect any alien civilizations.

80. In the search for life, scientists analyze not only biological but also technological traces, such as potential megastructures in space.

81. The Solar System formed about 4.6 billion years ago from a cloud of gas and dust.

82. The Sun accounts for 99.86% of the total mass of the Solar System.

83. Mercury, the planet closest to the Sun, experiences extreme temperatures ranging from -173°C (-280°F) at night to 427°C (800°F) during the day.

84. Venus rotates in the opposite direction to most planets in the Solar System.

85. Earth is the only planet known to support life and has active tectonic plates.

86. Mars is known as the "Red Planet" due to iron oxide giving it its distinctive color.

87. Mars hosts Olympus Mons, the tallest known mountain in the Solar System, standing 21 kilometers (13 miles) high.

88. The asteroid belt between Mars and Jupiter contains hundreds of thousands of rocky objects, the largest of which is the dwarf planet Ceres.

89. Jupiter, the largest planet in the Solar System, has over 75 moons, including Ganymede – the largest moon in the Solar System.

90. The Great Red Spot on Jupiter is a massive storm that has lasted for at least 350 years.

91. Saturn is famous for its rings, which are primarily made of ice and small rocky particles.

92. Uranus is the only planet that rotates "on its side," with an axial tilt of 98 degrees.

93. Neptune, the farthest planet from the Sun, has the strongest winds in the Solar System, reaching speeds of 2,100 km/h (1,300 mph).

94. Pluto, once considered the ninth planet, is now classified as a dwarf planet.

95. The dwarf planet Eris, located beyond Pluto, is slightly smaller but more massive than Pluto.

96. Comets, such as the famous Halley's Comet, are icy objects originating from the Oort Cloud and Kuiper Belt.

97. The Voyager 1 and Voyager 2 probes are the farthest human-made objects and are now exploring interstellar space.

98. The so-called "Ninth Planet" is a hypothetical object whose existence is suggested by irregularities in the orbits of some Kuiper Belt objects.

99. In its final stage of life, the Sun will become a red giant, engulfing the inner planets, including Earth.

100. The Kuiper Belt beyond Neptune's orbit contains numerous icy bodies, one of which is Pluto.

Chapter 2: The Astonishing Properties of Earth

1. Earth's Atmosphere and Its Wonders

101. Earth's atmosphere consists of five main layers: the troposphere, stratosphere, mesosphere, thermosphere, and exosphere.

102. The troposphere, the lowest layer, is where most weather phenomena occur.

103. The ozone layer in the stratosphere protects Earth from harmful ultraviolet radiation.

104. Without the atmosphere, Earth's temperatures would range from -150°C (-238°F) to 120°C (248°F), making life impossible.

105. Earth's atmosphere is composed primarily of nitrogen (78%) and oxygen (21%), with small amounts of other gases like argon and carbon dioxide.

106. Auroras, known as the northern and southern lights (aurora borealis and aurora australis), form when solar wind particles collide with atmospheric particles.

107. Earth's atmosphere acts as a giant filter, scattering sunlight and giving the sky its blue color.

108. Clouds form from the condensation of water vapor in the troposphere and appear in various shapes, such as cirrus, cumulus, and stratus.

109. The highest clouds on Earth, noctilucent clouds, form in the mesosphere at altitudes of about 80 km (50 miles).

110. The atmosphere serves as a protective shield, burning up most meteoroids before they can impact Earth's surface.

111. Sea-level atmospheric pressure is approximately 1013 hPa (hectopascals) and decreases with altitude.

112. The thermosphere can reach temperatures of over 2000°C (3632°F) due to the absorption of solar radiation.

113. Carbon dioxide and methane in the atmosphere act as greenhouse gases, maintaining Earth's temperature at life-supporting levels.

114. Earth experiences a carbon cycle in which carbon dioxide is absorbed and released by the atmosphere, oceans, plants, and soils.

115. Earth's atmosphere is unique in the Solar System for its oxygen content and the presence of liquid water.

116. High atmospheric pressure can result in stable weather conditions, while low pressure is often associated with storms.

117. Phenomena such as rainbows and halos occur due to the refraction, reflection, and dispersion of light in the atmosphere.

118. Earth's atmosphere continuously loses small amounts of gas to space, but this process is very slow and does not threaten life.

119. Research balloons in the stratosphere gather data on atmospheric composition and global climate changes.

120. Earth's atmosphere acts as a thermal insulator, preventing rapid cooling of the surface at night.

2. Incredible Geological Phenomena

121. Earthquakes result from the movement of tectonic plates and the release of energy stored in Earth's crust.

122. The largest recorded earthquake occurred in Chile in 1960, with a magnitude of 9.5.

123. Volcanoes form where magma reaches the surface, typically at tectonic plate boundaries.

124. The Krakatoa volcanic eruption in 1883 was so powerful that its sound was heard up to 4,800 km (3,000 miles) away.

125. Geysers, such as Old Faithful in Yellowstone National Park, erupt with hot water and steam when groundwater is heated by magma.

126. Tectonic plate movements are responsible for forming mountains like the Himalayas, which continue to grow by a few millimeters annually.

127. Ocean trenches, such as the Mariana Trench, form where one tectonic plate is subducted beneath another.

128. Earth's magnetic field, known as the geomagnetic field, is generated by the movement of liquid iron in Earth's core.

129. Shifting sand dunes, like those in the Sahara, change shape and location due to wind activity.

130. Glaciers slowly move across Earth's surface, shaping landscapes by carving U-shaped valleys and forming glacial lakes.

131. Crater lakes, such as Crater Lake in the USA, form when volcanoes collapse after eruptions.

132. The phenomenon of "firefalls," such as in Yosemite National Park, occurs when sunlight hits falling water at the right angle.

133. Auroras can also appear underground, known as subterranean auroras, visible in caves due to the fluorescence of minerals.

134. Desert roses are crystal formations of gypsum or barite that resemble the petals of a rose.

135. Mountain folding creates dramatic landforms like the Alps or Andes through the compression of tectonic plates.

136. Mud volcanoes erupt mud and gas instead of magma and are often associated with underground oil reservoirs.

137. Karst caves, such as Postojna Cave in Slovenia, are formed by the dissolution of limestone by water.

138. Devil's Towers, like the one in Wyoming, were formed by the erosion of surrounding rock, exposing massive volcanic intrusions.

139. Tsunamis, giant waves caused by underwater earthquakes or volcanic eruptions, can travel at speeds exceeding 800 km/h (500 mph).

140. Volcanic islands, such as Hawaii, form over "hot spots," stationary sources of magma beneath Earth's crust.

3. Extreme Places on Earth

141. The highest point on Earth is Mount Everest in the Himalayas, rising to an elevation of 8,848.86 meters (29,031.7 feet) above sea level.

142. The deepest place on Earth is the Mariana Trench in the Pacific Ocean, with its lowest point, Challenger Deep, at a depth of about 10,984 meters (36,037 feet).

143. The hottest place on Earth is Death Valley in California, where a record temperature of 56.7°C (134°F) was recorded in 1913.

144. The coldest place on Earth is the Vostok research station in Antarctica, where a temperature of -89.2°C (-128.6°F) was recorded in 1983.

145. Antarctica is the windiest place on Earth, with wind speeds exceeding 320 km/h (200 mph).

146. The rainiest place in the world is Mawsynram, India, with annual rainfall exceeding 11,871 mm (467.4 inches).

147. The driest place on Earth is the Atacama Desert in Chile, where some areas have gone centuries without rainfall.

148. The deepest lake on Earth is Lake Baikal in Russia, reaching a depth of 1,642 meters (5,387 feet) and containing about 20% of the world's freshwater reserves.

149. The tallest waterfall in the world is Angel Falls in Venezuela, with a height of 979 meters (3,212 feet).

150. Salar de Uyuni in Bolivia is the largest salt flat on Earth, covering over 10,000 square kilometers (3,900 square miles).

151. The Great Barrier Reef off the coast of Australia is the largest biological structure on Earth, visible from space.

152. Mauna Kea in Hawaii is the tallest volcano on Earth when measured from its base on the ocean floor, with a total height of over 10,200 meters (33,500 feet).

153. The oldest known rocks on Earth, found in Canada, are approximately 4 billion years old.

154. The most radioactive place on Earth is the Chernobyl Exclusion Zone, though nature is beginning to recover there.

155. Yungay in the Atacama Desert is one of the most inhospitable places for life, often used to simulate Martian conditions.

156. The deepest mine in the world, Mponeng in South Africa, extends over 4 kilometers (2.5 miles) below the Earth's surface.

157. Antarctica contains the largest concentration of glaciers, holding about 90% of the world's ice.

158. The most active volcano in the world is Kilauea in Hawaii, which has been erupting almost continuously since 1983.

159. Tristan da Cunha, an island in the South Atlantic, is the most remote inhabited island on Earth, with the nearest land over 2,400 kilometers (1,500 miles) away.

160. The largest cave in the world, Sơn Đoòng in Vietnam, is so massive it contains its own ecosystem and a river.

4. Water – The Source of Life

161. Water covers approximately 71% of Earth's surface, with 97% being salty water in the oceans.

162. Only 3% of the global water supply is freshwater, most of which is trapped in glaciers and ice caps.

163. Water is the only substance on Earth that naturally exists in all three states: liquid, solid, and gas.

164. Water has the unique property of expanding when freezing, causing ice to float on its surface.

165. About 60% of the human body is composed of water, with the brain containing up to 75%.

166. Every person needs about 2-3 liters of water daily to maintain proper bodily functions.

167. The ocean serves as the primary reservoir of water and thermal energy, influencing global climate.

168. Water molecules on Earth are incredibly old, possibly as ancient as 4.6 billion years.

169. Water is one of the best solvents, essential for life by enabling chemical reactions in organisms.

170. The water cycle includes evaporation, condensation, precipitation, and surface runoff.

171. The Amazon River is the largest river on Earth by water flow, contributing about 20% of the world's freshwater discharge into the ocean.

172. Lake Baikal in Russia holds the largest volume of liquid freshwater globally, accounting for about 20% of the world's supply.

173. Seawater is rich in minerals such as sodium, magnesium, and potassium, which sustain ocean ecosystems.

174. In extreme places like Death Valley, water in puddles can evaporate within minutes due to high heat and aridity.

175. Algae in the oceans produce over 50% of Earth's oxygen, making water a critical component of biological processes.

176. Deep oceans conceal vast reservoirs of water in the form of methane hydrates, which could become a future energy source.

177. Ocean currents, such as the Gulf Stream, significantly influence global climate and weather patterns.

178. The Moon's gravity causes ocean tides, helping regulate coastal ecosystems.

179. Freshwater is one of the planet's most limited resources – around 2 billion people worldwide lack access to safe drinking water.

180. Solar desalination of water is one of the oldest techniques for obtaining freshwater, used as far back as ancient times.

5. Evolution and Climate Change

181. Earth's climate has changed naturally over billions of years, transitioning through ice ages and warmer periods.

182. In the past, atmospheric carbon dioxide levels were much higher, such as during the Cretaceous period.

183. During the Pleistocene epoch (around 2.5 million years ago), numerous ice ages occurred, influencing the evolution of humans and animals.

184. Global warming caused by human activity is driving climate changes at a faster rate than natural processes.

185. Melting glaciers contribute to rising sea levels, threatening many coastal cities worldwide.

186. Mass extinctions in Earth's history, such as the Permian extinction, were associated with abrupt climate changes.

187. Volcanoes release large amounts of carbon dioxide and sulfur into the atmosphere, which can either cool or warm the climate.

188. The Tambora volcanic eruption in 1815 caused the "Year Without a Summer" due to ash blocking sunlight.

189. Oceans absorb about 25% of human-emitted carbon dioxide, leading to ocean acidification.

190. An increase of just 1.5°C in Earth's average temperature could cause irreversible damage to ecosystems.

191. Climate change affects species migration as animals and plants move to find suitable climatic conditions.

192. Coral reefs, such as the Great Barrier Reef, are especially vulnerable to rising ocean temperatures and acidification.

193. Arctic warming is causing permafrost to thaw, releasing methane – a potent greenhouse gas.

194. In the last 100 years, sea levels have risen by about 20 cm (8 inches), with the rate of increase accelerating.

195. Human impact on the climate became significant during the Industrial Revolution, when fossil fuel combustion became widespread.

196. Climate models predict more frequent and intense heatwaves, hurricanes, and floods in the future.

197. Deforestation reduces natural carbon dioxide sinks, exacerbating the greenhouse effect.

198. An increasing number of countries are investing in renewable energy sources, such as solar and wind power, to reduce greenhouse gas emissions.

199. International agreements like the Paris Agreement aim to limit global warming to 1.5°C above pre-industrial levels.

200. Climate change affects not only the environment but also human health, increasing the incidence of heat-related illnesses, drought-related issues, and air pollution.

Chapter 3: Biological Phenomena

1. Genetics – The Code of Life

201. DNA (deoxyribonucleic acid) is the molecule that stores the genetic information of all living organisms.

202. The human genome contains approximately 3 billion base pairs, 99.9% of which are identical among all humans.

203. DNA is composed of four nitrogenous bases: adenine (A), thymine (T), cytosine (C), and guanine (G), which form complementary pairs (A-T, C-G).

204. Human DNA is organized into 23 pairs of chromosomes, with half inherited from the mother and half from the father.

205. Genes are segments of DNA that code for proteins, which perform various functions in organisms.

206. Mutations in DNA can result in new traits or genetic disorders.

207. The human body contains approximately 37 trillion cells, each carrying a complete set of genetic information.

208. RNA (ribonucleic acid) acts as an intermediary, transferring information from DNA to the cellular machinery that produces proteins.

209. The "Human Genome Project," completed in 2003, mapped the entire human genome, paving the way for medical breakthroughs.

210. Mitochondria, known as the "powerhouses of cells," have their own DNA, which is inherited exclusively from the mother.

211. Telomeres, structures at the ends of chromosomes, protect DNA from damage but shorten with age, contributing to the aging process.

212. Every cell in the body, except for sex cells, contains the same DNA, even though they perform different functions.

213. Cloning, such as the creation of Dolly the sheep in 1996, uses genetics to produce genetically identical organisms.

214. Genes determine hereditary traits such as eye color, height, and susceptibility to certain diseases.

215. Only about 2% of human DNA codes for proteins – the rest is non-coding DNA, which performs other regulatory functions.

216. The genome of some plants, such as wheat, is much larger than the human genome, containing up to 17 billion base pairs.

217. Genetics plays a crucial role in personalized medicine, allowing treatments to be tailored to individual patient needs.

218. Through genetic modifications (GMOs), scientists create organisms with enhanced traits, such as increased disease resistance or higher crop yields.

219. Genes significantly influence behavior, intelligence, and temperament, but their effects are also shaped by environmental factors.

220. CRISPR-Cas9 is a groundbreaking gene-editing technology that allows precise changes to DNA, opening new possibilities for treating genetic disorders.

2. Fascinating Animal Abilities

221. Dolphins can recognize themselves in mirrors, indicating a high level of self-awareness.

222. Octopuses have three hearts and can change the color and texture of their skin, allowing them to blend seamlessly with their surroundings.

223. Dogs can detect diseases such as cancer by sensing changes in a person's body odor.

224. Pigeons can perceive Earth's magnetic fields, helping them navigate during migration.

225. Hummingbirds can flap their wings up to 80 times per second, enabling them to hover in place.

226. Cuttlefish can mimic the shapes and colors of their surroundings in a fraction of a second, making them masters of camouflage.

227. Bats use echolocation to navigate in the dark, emitting ultrasonic sounds and interpreting their echoes to avoid obstacles.

228. Migratory birds, such as storks, travel thousands of miles using the position of the Sun and stars for navigation.

229. Spiders spin silk webs that are five times stronger than steel of the same thickness.

230. Sharks have an organ called the ampullae of Lorenzini, allowing them to detect the electric fields emitted by other organisms.

231. Chameleons can move each eye independently, enabling them to observe different parts of their surroundings simultaneously.

232. Elephants communicate over long distances using infrasound, which is inaudible to the human ear.

233. Some lizard species can regenerate lost tails, a defense mechanism against predators.

234. Crows and ravens can solve complex problems and are considered some of the most intelligent birds.

235. Sea turtles return to the same beaches where they hatched to lay their eggs, even after years of traveling the oceans.

236. Domestic cats can hear higher frequency sounds than dogs, making them excellent hunters.

237. Kangaroos use their tails as a fifth limb, aiding in balance and jumping.

238. Ants can form living bridges with their bodies to cross gaps and obstacles collectively.

239. Emperor penguins survive Antarctica's extreme cold thanks to specialized feather structures and insulating fat.

240. Predatory wasps, such as tarantula hawks, paralyze their prey and lay eggs inside, where the larvae feed on the living host.

3. Plants That Amaze

241. Bamboo is the fastest-growing plant in the world, capable of growing up to 91 cm (36 inches) in a single day.

242. Rafflesia arnoldii, known as the "corpse flower," has the largest single flower in the world, measuring up to 1 meter (3.3 feet) in diameter.

243. Welwitschia mirabilis, native to the Namib Desert, can live up to 2,000 years and only ever grows two leaves throughout its life.

244. The Venus flytrap, a carnivorous plant, can snap its traps shut in just 0.1 seconds to catch its prey.

245. The giant sequoia tree named "General Sherman" in California is the largest tree by volume in the world.

246. Pitcher plants of the genus Nepenthes create liquid-filled traps to drown and digest insects.

247. The baobab tree can store up to 120,000 liters (31,700 gallons) of water in its trunk, helping it survive droughts.

248. Sundews attract insects with a sweet substance, then wrap their sticky leaves around them to digest them.

249. Water lotus flowers are self-cleaning, thanks to a unique surface structure that repels water and dirt.

250. Wolffia, a type of watermeal, is the smallest flowering plant in the world, measuring just 0.5 mm.

251. Olive trees can live for thousands of years, with the oldest known olive tree being around 3,000 years old and still bearing fruit.

252. Orchids of the genus Ophrys mimic the appearance and scent of insects to attract pollinators.

253. Weeping willows can reproduce simply by planting a branch in the ground, where it will root and grow into a new tree.

254. Red algae, such as Porphyra, are eaten as nori and are rich in protein and vitamins.

255. The dragon tree of the Canary Islands produces a red sap known as "dragon's blood," historically used as a dye and medicine.

256. The telegraph plant (Desmodium gyrans) moves its leaves in response to light or sound, creating a "dancing" effect.

257. Cycads, among the oldest plant species, have existed for over 300 million years, predating the dinosaurs.

258. Water hyacinth is the fastest-spreading aquatic plant, capable of covering entire lakes within weeks.

259. The resurrection plant, or Rose of Jericho, can survive complete desiccation and revive when exposed to water.

4. Microorganisms – Invisible Wonders

260. Microorganisms, such as bacteria, viruses, fungi, and protozoa, are the smallest yet most numerous forms of life on Earth.

261. One gram of soil contains about a billion bacteria and thousands of species of microorganisms.

262. Escherichia coli (E. coli) bacteria can divide every 20 minutes, making them among the fastest-reproducing organisms.

263. Viruses, such as HIV and the flu virus, are not considered living organisms because they cannot reproduce independently.

264. Yeasts, which are microorganisms, have been used in baking and brewing for thousands of years.

265. Archaea, which resemble bacteria, can survive extreme conditions like hot springs and salty lakes.

266. Mitochondria, the "powerhouses" of cells, originated from ancient bacteria that entered into symbiosis with eukaryotic cells.

267. Microorganisms play a key role in the nitrogen cycle, converting atmospheric nitrogen into forms usable by plants.

268. Bioluminescent bacteria make some marine animals, such as squids, glow in the dark.

269. Microorganisms also live within our bodies – there are more in the human gut than cells in the entire body.

270. In 2016, the Mollivirus sibericum virus was discovered in 30,000-year-old permafrost and was still capable of infection.

271. Some microorganisms, like Deinococcus radiodurans, can survive extreme radiation, even in outer space.

272. Antibiotics, such as penicillin, are produced by microorganisms like fungi as a defense mechanism against bacteria.

273. Phytoplankton, microscopic marine organisms, produce about 50% of the oxygen on Earth.

274. The human microbiome, microorganisms living on the skin and within the body, protects against infections and aids digestion.

275. Microorganisms are used in biotechnology, such as for producing insulin and breaking down environmental pollutants.

276. Some bacteria, like Geobacter, can generate electricity by converting organic substances into energy.

277. Microorganisms have been found in clouds and can influence the formation of rain and snow.

278. The oldest fossilized bacteria are estimated to be about 3.5 billion years old, making them among the earliest forms of life on Earth.

5. The Human Body by the Numbers

279. The human body is made up of approximately 37 trillion cells.

280. The human heart beats an average of 100,000 times per day, pumping around 7,570 liters (2,000 gallons) of blood.

281. The total length of blood vessels in the human body is about 100,000 kilometers (62,000 miles).

282. The human brain contains approximately 86 billion neurons.

283. An adult breathes about 22,000 times a day, inhaling roughly 11,000 liters (2,900 gallons) of air.

284. The human skeleton is composed of 206 bones, 54 of which are in the hands.

285. The smallest bone in the human body is the stapes in the ear, measuring about 3 mm (0.12 inches) in length.

286. The skin, the largest organ in the body, weighs around 4 kg (8.8 pounds) and covers about 2 square meters (21.5 square feet).

287. Every day, the human body produces approximately 25 million new blood cells.

288. Hair grows an average of 1 cm (0.4 inches) per month, and a person loses about 50-100 hairs daily.

289. The small intestine of an adult is approximately 6 meters (20 feet) long.

290. The human liver performs over 500 functions, including detoxification and bile production.

291. The human body has about 640 muscles, which make up roughly 40% of its total mass.

292. Every day, the body produces about 1-1.5 liters (0.3-0.4 gallons) of saliva.

293. The kidneys process about 50 liters (13 gallons) of blood daily, producing approximately 1.5 liters (0.4 gallons) of urine.

294. The human stomach produces about 2 liters (0.5 gallons) of gastric acid each day to digest food.

295. The average human eye can distinguish about 10 million colors.

296. The human body hosts approximately 30 trillion bacteria, most of which are in the gut.

297. The average lifespan of a skin cell is about 28 days before being replaced by a new one.

298. Human blood moves at a speed of about 4-5 km/h (2.5-3.1 mph), circulating through the body in about one minute.

Chapter 4: Amazing Scientific Discoveries

1. Epoch-Making Inventions

299. The wheel, invented around 3500 BCE in ancient Mesopotamia, was one of humanity's most significant inventions. Initially used for pottery, it revolutionized transport by enabling the creation of carts and chariots.

300. Cuneiform writing, developed by the Sumerians around 3100 BCE, became the first writing system. It allowed for recording transactions, creating laws, and documenting history, advancing civilization.

301. The compass, invented in 9th-century China, transformed maritime navigation, allowing precise travel under any weather conditions and enabling the exploration of new continents.

302. The printing press, created by Johannes Gutenberg in 1440, facilitated mass production of books, accelerating knowledge, scientific advancement, and religious reform.

303. The microscope, invented by Zacharias Janssen in the early 17th century, unveiled the microscopic world, advancing biology, medicine, and microbiology.

304. The steam engine, improved by James Watt in the 18th century, ignited the Industrial Revolution. It revolutionized transport (trains, ships) and industry, boosting production efficiency.

305. The electric light bulb, invented by Thomas Edison in 1879, illuminated cities and homes, extending work and social activities while driving global electrification.

306. The telephone, invented by Alexander Graham Bell in 1876, enabled instant long-distance communication, transforming personal and business interactions.

307. The airplane, first successfully flown by the Wright brothers in 1903, opened the era of aviation, making the world more connected and accessible.

308. Penicillin, discovered accidentally by Alexander Fleming in 1928, became the first antibiotic, saving millions of lives and ushering in modern medicine.

309. Computers, such as ENIAC built in 1945, were room-sized devices that laid the foundation for today's personal computers, revolutionizing work and communication.

310. The internet, developed in the 1960s as ARPANET, was initially a military tool. By the 1990s, it became a global medium, transforming access to information, education, and communication.

311. Lasers, invented by Theodore Maiman in 1960, found applications in medicine, communication, entertainment, and industry, becoming ubiquitous in everyday life.

312. GPS (Global Positioning System), introduced in the 1970s by the U.S. Department of Defense, became an indispensable tool for navigation, logistics, and exploration.

313. Vaccines, first used by Edward Jenner in 1796 against smallpox, have saved billions from infectious diseases. Innovations like COVID-19 vaccines highlight their vital role in public health.

314. Robotics, with the first industrial robots introduced in the 1960s, revolutionized manufacturing. Today, robotics encompasses autonomous vehicles, medical robots, and home assistants.

315. Nuclear energy, enabled by discoveries in atomic fission in the 1930s, became one of the most efficient energy sources.

316. 3D printing, invented in the 1980s, allows the creation of items ranging from medical implants to car parts with minimal waste.

317. CRISPR-Cas9, discovered in 2012, is a gene-editing system enabling precise DNA modifications, opening new frontiers in medicine, agriculture, and biological research.

2. The Most Surprising Experiments

319. The Miller-Urey Experiment (1953) – Simulating Earth's primordial atmosphere, it demonstrated that simple chemical compounds could form amino acids, the building blocks of life.

320. Schrödinger's Cat Experiment (1935) – Erwin Schrödinger's thought experiment illustrated the paradoxes of quantum mechanics, showing the concept of superposition in the microscopic world.

321. The Philadelphia Experiment (1943) – Allegedly involving the teleportation of a naval ship, this story, though considered a myth, inspired studies in quantum teleportation.

322. Harlow's Monkey Experiment (1958) – Research on attachment showed that young monkeys preferred soft "mothers" over metal ones providing food, profoundly impacting child psychology.

323. Milgram's Obedience Experiment (1961) – Revealed that people are willing to inflict harm on others under authority orders, even against their personal beliefs.

324. The Stanford Prison Experiment (1971) – Philip Zimbardo's study demonstrated how quickly people adopt roles like guards and prisoners, leading to extreme behaviors. It was terminated due to ethical concerns.

325. NASA Twin Study (2015–2016) – Astronaut Scott Kelly spent a year in space while his twin, Mark Kelly, remained on Earth. The study revealed the effects of long-term space travel on the human body.

326. Foucault's Pendulum Experiment (1851) – Léon Foucault used a pendulum to visually confirm Earth's rotation, providing a groundbreaking observable demonstration.

327. Rat Park Experiment (1978) – Bruce Alexander showed that addiction heavily depends on the environment, transforming perspectives on addiction treatment.

328. Little Albert Experiment (1920) – John B. Watson demonstrated that fear could be conditioned, though the experiment raised significant ethical concerns.

329. Luria-Delbrück Experiment (1943) – Showed that genetic mutations occur randomly rather than being induced by environmental factors, a milestone in genetics.

330. Pavlov's Classical Conditioning (1890s) – Ivan Pavlov's studies on dogs salivating at a bell's sound revolutionized behavioral psychology.

331. Asch Conformity Experiment (1951) – Solomon Asch revealed that individuals often conform to group opinions, even when those opinions are incorrect.

332. The Double-Slit Experiment (1801) – Thomas Young demonstrated that light exhibits both wave and particle properties, laying the groundwork for quantum theory.

333. Halliwell-Roser Plant Memory Experiment (2013) – Discovered that plants "remember" stressful experiences and adapt, suggesting a form of plant "intelligence."

334. Microbe Survival in Space Experiment (2020) – Demonstrated that microorganisms can survive in a vacuum, supporting the panspermia theory that life might have come to Earth from space.

335. Boyle's Law Experiment (1660) – Robert Boyle showed that gas pressure is inversely proportional to its volume, foundational for thermodynamics.

336. Rutherford's Gold Foil Experiment (1909) – Bombarding thin gold foil with alpha particles revealed the atomic nucleus, revolutionizing our understanding of matter.

337. Lenski's Long-Term Evolution Experiment (1988–Present) – Studies show how quickly bacteria adapt to changing conditions, providing evidence of microevolution.

3. Brilliant Mistakes That Changed the World

338. Penicillin (1928) – Alexander Fleming discovered the first antibiotic by accident when he noticed that Penicillium mold inhibited bacterial growth on a forgotten petri dish.

339. Microwaves and the Microwave Oven (1945) – Percy Spencer noticed that a chocolate bar in his pocket melted while working with a magnetron, leading to the invention of the microwave oven.

340. X-rays (1895) – Wilhelm Roentgen accidentally discovered X-rays during experiments with cathode rays, revolutionizing medicine.

341. Teflon (1938) – Roy Plunkett discovered Teflon when tetrafluoroethylene gas unexpectedly turned into a slippery solid, now widely used in cookware and industry.

342. Superglue (1942) – Harry Coover unintentionally invented cyanoacrylate while developing a clear plastic for military use, but it turned out to be an exceptional adhesive.

343. Insulin (1921) – Frederick Banting and Charles Best discovered insulin after seemingly failed experiments on dogs led to identifying the hormone that regulates blood sugar.

344. LSD (1938) – Albert Hofmann discovered the psychedelic properties of LSD accidentally when the substance absorbed through his skin during painkiller research.

345. Pacemaker (1956) – Wilson Greatbatch inadvertently used the wrong resistor in a circuit, which led to the invention of the first implantable heart pacemaker.

346. Synthetic Dyes (1856) – William Perkin discovered the first synthetic dye, mauveine, while attempting to create a malaria treatment, sparking the chemical industry.

347. Viagra (1998) – Originally developed as a medication for hypertension, it was found effective in treating erectile dysfunction, becoming its primary use.

348. Stainless Steel (1913) – Harry Brearley accidentally created stainless steel while experimenting with corrosion-resistant alloys for the arms industry.

349. Dynamite (1867) – Alfred Nobel stabilized nitroglycerin by combining it with diatomaceous earth, creating a safe explosive with applications in construction and mining.

350. Post-it Notes (1968) – Spencer Silver invented a weak adhesive that turned out perfect for sticky notes, despite initially aiming for a stronger glue.

351. Corn Flakes (1894) – The Kellogg brothers accidentally invented breakfast cereal when cooked wheat was left out, hardened, and turned into crisp flakes after processing.

352. Plastic (1907) – Leo Baekeland unintentionally created Bakelite, the first synthetic plastic, initiating the age of plastics.

353. Fluorescence in Fish (1960s) – Scientists studying jellyfish genes discovered green fluorescent protein, revolutionizing biological research.

354. Potato Chips (1853) – George Crum created potato chips in frustration when a customer complained about thick fries, frying thin slices into crispy snacks.

355. Scotch Tape (1930) – Richard Drew developed adhesive tape initially for painters, but it became an essential office supply.

356. Computed Tomography (CT) (1972) – Engineers at EMI, originally working on seismic analysis devices, accidentally invented the CT scanner, transforming medical diagnostics.

357. Penicillin in Veterinary Medicine (1930s) – Early tests of the antibiotic on livestock revealed its effectiveness in improving animal health and growth, impacting agriculture.

4. Unresolved Mysteries of Science

358. What is dark matter? – Estimated to account for about 27% of the universe's mass, the nature of dark matter remains unknown.

359. What is dark energy? – Responsible for the accelerating expansion of the universe, dark energy makes up about 68% of the cosmos, yet its mechanisms are unclear.

360. What happened at the beginning of the universe? – While the Big Bang theory explains the universe's evolution, what occurred in the first fractions of a second or what existed before remains a mystery.

361. How did life originate? – Despite advances in biology, we still don't know how non-living chemical compounds transformed into the first forms of life.

362. Does life exist beyond Earth? – The search for life on Mars, Europa, Enceladus, and exoplanets is one of science's most pressing questions.

363. How does consciousness work? – The mechanisms that create human consciousness and subjective experience remain a mystery for neuroscience and psychology.

364. Why does time flow in one direction? – The arrow of time, tied to entropy, raises questions about why the past and future are asymmetrical.

365. What are the boundaries of the universe? – It's unknown whether the universe is infinite or has a defined size and shape.

366. Is time travel possible? – While spacetime might theoretically allow for time travel, there's no evidence to support its feasibility.

367. Do other universes exist? – The multiverse theory suggests our universe is one of many, but no evidence has been found to confirm this.

368. What is gravity at the quantum level? – While gravity is well understood on large scales, its quantum nature remains unresolved.

369. What happens inside a black hole? – The extreme gravity in black holes defies our current models of physics.

370. How does collective consciousness form? – Phenomena like swarm behavior in insects or brain synchronization in groups are still poorly understood.

371. Why do humans dream? – While the mechanisms of sleep are known, the purpose and function of dreams remain elusive.

372. How did the largest structures in the universe form? – Galaxy clusters and cosmic filaments are not yet fully understood in the context of the universe's evolution.

373. Do supersymmetric particles exist? – Supersymmetry predicts partners for known particles, but none have been observed so far.

374. Do animals have consciousness? – Research continues into the extent to which animals experience emotions, memory, and self-awareness.

375. Why is the universe asymmetric? – Matter and antimatter should exist in equal amounts, yet matter dominates the universe.

376. What causes Earth's magnetic field? – While it shields us from cosmic radiation, the exact mechanisms of its generation are still under study.

377. Are the laws of physics universal? – It's uncertain whether the known laws of physics operate the same way in distant regions of the universe.

5. Technologies of the Future

378. Artificial Intelligence (AI) – In the future, AI could take over tasks ranging from medical diagnostics to city management, raising ethical and control-related questions.

379. Quantum Computing – Based on quantum mechanics, it may revolutionize computing by solving problems currently impossible for classical computers.

380. Nanotechnology – Manipulating matter at the atomic level could revolutionize medicine, for example, by creating nanorobots capable of repairing damaged cells.

381. Augmented Reality (AR) – AR will integrate virtual elements into the real world, transforming education, entertainment, and the way we work.

382. 3D Bioprinting – Future 3D printers could create human organs, revolutionizing transplantation and regenerative medicine.

383. Blockchain Technologies – Expanding blockchain beyond cryptocurrencies to supply chain management or data storage could make transactions more transparent and secure.

384. Autonomous Vehicles – Self-driving cars and drones could reduce traffic accidents, improve public transport, and revolutionize logistics.

385. Green Energy – New energy storage technologies, such as lithium-sulfur batteries, could make renewable energy more efficient and accessible.

386. Nuclear Fusion – Projects like ITER aim to create efficient fusion reactors, potentially providing an inexhaustible energy source.

387. Lab-Grown Meat – Producing meat in laboratories could reduce greenhouse gas emissions and minimize animal suffering.

388. Space Technologies – Advancements like SpaceX's Starship or the Lunar Gateway are bringing us closer to colonizing the Moon and Mars.

389. Internet of Things (IoT) – Connected devices could make our homes and cities smarter but also increase the risk of cyberattacks.

390. Gene Editing (CRISPR) – Gene-editing technology could enable cures for genetic diseases, improve crops, and extend human lifespan.

391. Flexible and Holographic Displays – Future holographic screens might replace traditional monitors, offering new ways to interact with technology.

392. Virtual Simulations – Virtual reality (VR) could revolutionize medical, military, and professional training with realistic simulations.

393. Maglev Transportation – Trains levitating on magnetic tracks could achieve speeds over 600 km/h (373 mph), making travel faster and greener.

394. Agricultural Technologies – Vertical farming and agricultural robots could transform food production to meet the needs of a growing population.

395. Future Cybersecurity – As quantum technologies evolve, new security systems could replace traditional encryption methods.

396. Quantum Teleportation – Currently limited to particles, teleportation may one day enable data transmission over unimaginable distances.

397. Extreme Preventive Medicine – Real-time health monitoring technologies could detect diseases before symptoms appear, revolutionizing early intervention.

Chapter 5: Wonders of Physics

1. Quantum Oddities

398. Superposition – Particles can exist in multiple states or locations simultaneously until measured, as illustrated by Schrödinger's cat thought experiment.

399. Quantum Entanglement – Two particles can become "entangled," meaning a change in one instantly affects the state of the other, even if separated by billions of kilometers.

400. Wave-Particle Duality – Particles like electrons and photons behave as both waves and particles, depending on how they are observed.

401. Tunneling Effect – Quantum particles can "tunnel" through energy barriers that would normally be impassable, a phenomenon utilized in transistors.

402. Heisenberg's Uncertainty Principle – It is impossible to precisely measure both the position and momentum of a particle at the same time, a cornerstone of quantum mechanics.

403. Casimir Effect – Quantum vacuum fluctuations can generate an attractive force between objects placed very close together.

404. Virtual Particles – Virtual particles continuously appear and vanish in a vacuum, affecting real-world physical phenomena despite their fleeting existence.

405. Vacuum Fluctuations – At the quantum scale, empty space is never truly empty but is filled with constant energy fluctuations.

406. Double-Slit Experiment – Demonstrates that particles can pass through two slits simultaneously, creating an interference pattern as if they were waves.

407. Quantum Tunneling in Stars – Tunneling is essential for nuclear reactions in stars, enabling hydrogen to fuse into helium.

408. Time in Quantum Mechanics – At the quantum level, time may be discontinuous, with events occurring in "jumps."

409. Quantum Decoherence – When particles interact with their environment, they lose their quantum properties and begin behaving classically.

410. Zeno Effect – Observing a quantum system can halt its changes, highlighting the peculiarities of quantum mechanics.

411. Quantum Computing – Quantum computers use superposition and entanglement to perform calculations impossible for traditional computers.

412. Quantum Gravity – Scientists are still working to unify gravity with quantum mechanics, one of the biggest puzzles in physics.

413. Unruh Effect – An accelerating observer in a quantum vacuum perceives the vacuum as hot, contrary to intuition.

414. Quantum Teleportation – Information about a quantum state can be transmitted over a distance using entanglement, though no matter is transported.

415. Ground State – Even at absolute zero, particles retain zero-point energy due to quantum fluctuations.

416. Quantum Spacetime – At the smallest scales, spacetime may resemble "quantum foam," with a dynamically fluctuating structure.

2. Relativity in Practice

417. Time slows down in motion – According to Einstein's special theory of relativity, the faster an object moves, the slower time flows for it relative to a stationary observer.

418. Atomic clock experiments – Time dilation was confirmed by sending atomic clocks aboard airplanes; their readings differed from those on Earth.

419. Gravitational time dilation – Time moves slower near massive objects like black holes, a phenomenon confirmed by experiments with GPS satellites.

420. Global Positioning System (GPS) – GPS satellites account for both special relativity (due to their speed) and general relativity (due to weaker gravity at their altitude) to provide accurate data.

421. Acceleration as a source of force – In accelerating frames, inertial forces arise, which, in relativity, result from spacetime curvature.

422. Gravitational lensing – Massive objects like galaxies bend light passing near them, enabling observations of distant cosmic phenomena.

423. Gravitational redshift – Light emitted near massive objects loses energy, shifting toward the red end of the electromagnetic spectrum.

424. Hafele-Keating Experiment (1971) – Atomic clocks on airplanes flying in opposite directions demonstrated relativistic effects on time.

425. Interstellar travel – At speeds approaching the speed of light, time passes more slowly for the traveler than for those on Earth, enabling "future travel."

426. Twin Paradox – A twin traveling at high speed in space ages more slowly than the one remaining on Earth.

427. Black holes – General relativity predicts that near a black hole's event horizon, time slows so much it nearly stops for a distant observer.

428. Interstellar and relativistic time – The film Interstellar illustrates gravitational time dilation, where proximity to a massive black hole makes one hour on a planet equivalent to seven years on Earth.

429. Pound-Rebka Experiment (1959) – Demonstrated gravitational time dilation in a lab by measuring changes in light frequency in Earth's gravitational field.

430. Light's path in curved spacetime – In general relativity, light follows the shortest path, or geodesic, which can appear as a curved trajectory.

431. Particle decay in accelerators – Particles moving near the speed of light live longer than stationary ones, confirming relativistic time dilation.

432. Einstein's equations – Describe how mass and energy affect spacetime geometry, leading to phenomena like black holes and gravitational lensing.

433. Radio signals from distant probes – Signals from probes like Voyager or New Horizons are delayed due to spacetime curvature near planets and the Sun.

434. Speed of light as a limit – In relativity, nothing can travel faster than light, as it would require infinite energy.

435. Blue shift – When an object approaches an observer, its light shifts toward the blue end of the spectrum, the opposite of the Doppler effect for sound.

3. Sound and Waves – The Invisible Power

436. Sound as a mechanical wave – It travels through solids, liquids, and gases as vibrations of particles but cannot move through a vacuum.

437. The speed of sound depends on the medium – In air, it travels at about 343 m/s, in water it's five times faster, and in steel, up to 15 times faster.

438. Standing waves – Found in enclosed spaces like musical instruments, they produce harmonic sounds.

439. Ultrasonics – Sound waves with frequencies above 20,000 Hz are inaudible to humans but are used in medicine (ultrasound) and navigation (echolocation).

440. Infrasound – Sound waves below 20 Hz can be felt as vibrations and are used to monitor earthquakes and volcanic eruptions.

441. Seismic waves – Sound waves traveling through the Earth during earthquakes provide insights into its internal structure.

442. Loud sounds – Volumes above 120 dB can cause pain, while 150 dB can result in permanent hearing damage.

443. Resonance – When an object vibrates at its natural frequency, resonance can occur, as seen in the collapse of the Tacoma Narrows Bridge in 1940.

444. Sound can "move" objects – Acoustic techniques like acoustic levitation use sound waves to suspend small objects in midair.

445. Sound underwater – Dolphins and whales use sound for communication and echolocation, and acoustic waves can travel great distances in oceans.

446. Ultrasound in technology – Used in industries for cutting materials, cleaning delicate surfaces, and in sonographic technologies.

447. Bat echolocation – Bats emit ultrasonic waves and analyze their echoes to navigate in complete darkness.

448. Sound waves in music – Each musical instrument has unique acoustic properties determined by its shape, material, and method of sound generation.

449. The sound barrier – Objects like airplanes that exceed the speed of sound create shock waves, producing a loud "sonic boom."

450. Sound in films – Surround sound technology leverages sound wave properties to create a sense of spatial audio.

451. Resonant frequencies of human organs – Sound waves at specific frequencies can influence parts of the body, used in sound therapy.

452. Sound and destruction – High frequencies and volumes can shatter glass by causing it to vibrate at its natural frequency.

453. Acoustic synesthesia – Some individuals experience seeing colors in response to sounds, a phenomenon studied in neurology and art.

454. Space exploration – Sounds in space are actually electromagnetic waves converted into audible frequencies, helping analyze planets and stars.

455. Underwater communication technology – Sonar uses sound waves to detect underwater objects, from shipwrecks to submarines.

4. Light and Optics

456. Light as both wave and particle – The wave-particle duality describes how light behaves as both an electromagnetic wave and discrete particles called photons.

457. Speed of light – In a vacuum, light travels at 299,792,458 m/s, making it the fastest known phenomenon in the universe.

458. Light dispersion – When passing through a prism, white light splits into different colors, forming a spectrum, a phenomenon discovered by Isaac Newton.

459. Light refraction – As light passes through different media, such as air to water, it changes direction, explaining why objects underwater appear closer.

460. Rainbows – Formed when sunlight refracts, reflects, and disperses in raindrops, creating colorful arcs in the sky.

461. Total internal reflection – When light moves from a denser to a rarer medium at the right angle, it is completely reflected, a principle used in fiber optics.

462. Diffraction – Light spreads out when passing through a narrow slit, creating interference patterns.

463. Polarization – Polarized light oscillates in a single plane, a property used in sunglasses to reduce glare.

464. Photons are massless – Although they have no mass, photons carry energy and momentum, allowing them to interact with matter.

465. Photoelectric effect – When light strikes metal, it can release electrons, a discovery that contributed to the development of quantum theory.

466. Lasers – Produce a coherent and focused beam of light through stimulated emission, with applications in medicine, telecommunications, and entertainment.

467. Lenses and magnification – Lenses in microscopes and telescopes refract light to magnify images of tiny or distant objects.

468. Doppler effect – When a light source moves toward an observer, its wavelength shortens (blue shift); when it moves away, the wavelength lengthens (red shift).

469. Aurora borealis and australis – The northern and southern lights occur when solar wind particles collide with atmospheric atoms, emitting photons.

470. Fiber optics – Use total internal reflection to transmit light over long distances, enabling high-speed data transfer.

471. Black holes and light – A black hole's gravity is so intense that it prevents light from escaping, rendering it invisible.

472. Light in medicine – Optical technologies like endoscopes and lasers enable precise diagnosis and treatment in healthcare.

473. Optical illusions – Occur when the brain interprets light and patterns differently from reality, revealing how we process visual information.

474. Dark energy and light – By analyzing light from distant supernovae, scientists discovered that the universe's expansion is accelerating, attributed to dark energy.

475. Future photonics – Using light in computing technology could replace traditional electrical circuits, significantly speeding up data processing.

5. Magnetic and Electrical Phenomena

476. Earth's magnetic field – Generated by the movement of liquid iron in Earth's core, it protects us from cosmic radiation and solar wind.

477. Aurora borealis and australis – These polar lights occur when solar wind particles collide with Earth's magnetic field, emitting light.

478. Electromagnetism – Links electricity and magnetism; the movement of electric charges generates a magnetic field.

479. Electromagnetic induction – Michael Faraday discovered that a changing magnetic field can generate an electric current, the principle behind generators.

480. Electric motor – Operates on the interaction between magnetic fields and electric currents, converting electrical energy into mechanical energy.

481. Transformer – Uses electromagnetic induction to change the voltage of electric current, essential for long-distance energy transmission.

482. Electrical conductivity – Materials like copper and silver are excellent conductors, while insulators like rubber block electrical flow.

483. Hall effect – When current flows through a conductor in a magnetic field, a perpendicular voltage is generated.

484. Magnetic field around current – Hans Christian Ørsted discovered that electric current produces a magnetic field around it.

485. Generators – Convert mechanical energy (e.g., from wind or water) into electrical energy, powering modern society.

486. Electromagnets – Coils of wire carrying electric current create temporary magnetic fields, used in devices like magnetic cranes.

487. Earth's magnetic poles – They are not fixed; they reverse approximately every 200,000–300,000 years, with the last reversal occurring 780,000 years ago.

488. Superconductivity – At low temperatures, some materials conduct electricity without resistance, enabling efficient superconducting magnets.

489. Permanent magnetism – Materials like neodymium magnets retain their magnetic fields without electrical power.

490. Electrical sparking – Occurs when potential differences are high enough to ionize air, creating sparks or lightning.

491. Lightning – Massive electrical discharges occur when potential differences between clouds and Earth reach millions of volts.

492. Coulomb's law – The force between two electric charges is directly proportional to the product of their charges and inversely proportional to the square of their distance.

493. Magnetism in animals – Species like sea turtles and migratory birds can detect Earth's magnetic fields for navigation.

494. Magnetic Resonance Imaging (MRI) – Uses strong magnetic fields and radio waves to create detailed internal body images, revolutionizing medical diagnostics.

495. Renewable energy and magnetism – Wind and hydroelectric power plants rely on magnetism in generators to produce clean energy.

Chapter 6: Chemistry in Everyday Life

1. Fascinating Properties of Elements

496. Hydrogen (H) – The lightest element, making up about 75% of the universe's mass. On Earth, it is a key component of water and essential for life.

497. Helium (He) – The second lightest element, used in balloons and cooling superconductors due to its resistance to liquefaction at near absolute zero temperatures.

498. Carbon (C) – The foundation of life on Earth, forming millions of organic compounds, including DNA, proteins, and sugars.

499. Oxygen (O) – Comprising 21% of Earth's atmosphere, it is vital for respiration and combustion, while in its ozone form, it protects against UV radiation.

500. Nitrogen (N) – The primary component of the atmosphere (78%) and a crucial element in proteins and nucleic acids in living organisms.

501. Iron (Fe) – Essential for oxygen transport in the blood (hemoglobin) and a key material in steel production.

502. Mercury (Hg) – The only metal that is liquid at room temperature, used in thermometers and barometers.

503. Sodium (Na) – Reacts violently with water; its compounds, like sodium chloride (table salt), are essential for life.

504. Chlorine (Cl) – A toxic gas, but in the form of salt (NaCl), it is vital for living organisms.

505. Gold (Au) – Highly durable and unreactive with most chemicals, it has been used for centuries as currency and ornamentation.

506. Uranium (U) – Fuels nuclear reactors and weapons, naturally occurring in the Earth's crust.

507. Silicon (Si) – The backbone of electronics (integrated circuits, solar panels) and the main component of sand and glass.

508. Fluorine (F) – The most reactive element, used in toothpaste and water fluoridation to prevent cavities.

509. Aluminum (Al) – A lightweight, strong, and corrosion-resistant metal used in aerospace and packaging industries.

510. Titanium (Ti) – As strong as steel but half the weight, it resists corrosion and is ideal for medical implants and aerospace applications.

511. Iodine (I) – Necessary for thyroid hormone production; its deficiency causes conditions like endemic goiter.

512. Arsenic (As) – Historically a poison, but it has applications in medicine and electronics, such as semiconductors.

513. Plutonium (Pu) – A key element in nuclear power and weaponry, though its radioactivity makes it extremely dangerous.

514. Lithium (Li) – Used in lithium-ion batteries, revolutionizing portable electronics and electric vehicles.

515. Neon (Ne) – Used in neon signs, glowing red-orange in a vacuum when exposed to electrical current.

2. Chemical Reactions in the Kitchen

516. Maillard Reaction – This occurs between amino acids and reducing sugars when heated, creating the characteristic flavor and color in meats, bread, and coffee.

517. Caramelization – Under high heat, sugars break down and transform, producing a distinctive brown color and sweet flavor.

518. Protein denaturation – When eggs are cooked, their proteins denature, changing structure and solidifying.

519. Acidic marinades – Acids like vinegar or lemon juice break down proteins in meat, making it more tender and flavorful.

520. Leavening dough – Baking soda (NaHCO₃) reacts with acids (like buttermilk) to produce carbon dioxide, making dough rise.

521. Gluten formation – In wheat flour, proteins glutenin and gliadin combine with water to form gluten, giving bread its elasticity.

522. Gelation – Gelatin or agar-agar binds water to form gels, used in jellies and desserts.

523. Emulsification – Sauces like mayonnaise are created when fat (oil) is dispersed in water using an emulsifier such as lecithin from egg yolks.

524. Fermentation – Yeast and bacteria convert sugars into alcohol and carbon dioxide, enabling the creation of bread, beer, and wine.

525. Enzymatic reactions – Enzymes in fruits, like papain in papaya, break down proteins in meat, tenderizing it.

526. Browning of fruits – Exposure to air causes oxidation of polyphenols in fruits like apples, turning them brown.

527. Milk coagulation – Adding acid to milk curdles casein proteins, forming the basis for cheese and curd.

528. Neutralization reaction – Adding baking soda to acidic foods like tomato sauce neutralizes acidity, enhancing flavor.

529. Melting and solidifying chocolate – Tempering chocolate controls the crystallization of cocoa butter, ensuring a smooth texture and shine.

530. Brine – Soaking meat in a salt solution causes osmotic absorption of water, increasing its juiciness.

531. Decarboxylation in spices – Toasting spices like coriander or cumin releases aromatic compounds, intensifying flavor.

532. Acid and pH effects – Adding lemon juice to seafood denatures proteins, "cooking" it without heat (as in ceviche).

533. Baking powder action – Contains baking soda, an acid, and a moisture absorber; it activates during baking, releasing gas.

534. Heating spices – High temperatures release essential oils from spices, enhancing aroma and flavor.

535. Fat oxidation – Fats in food can go rancid when exposed to oxygen, altering taste and smell; refrigeration or antioxidants help prevent this.

3. Substances That Changed the World

536. Gunpowder – Invented in 9th-century China, gunpowder revolutionized warfare by enabling the development of artillery and firearms.

537. Penicillin – Discovered by Alexander Fleming in 1928, it became the first antibiotic, saving millions of lives from bacterial infections.

538. Aspirin – Derived from willow bark, aspirin (acetylsalicylic acid) has been one of the most widely used pain relievers and anti-inflammatory drugs since the late 19th century.

539. Cement – Developed in the 19th century, Portland cement is the foundation of modern construction, enabling the rise of contemporary cities.

540. Nylon – Invented in 1935 by DuPont, nylon was the first synthetic fiber, widely used in clothing, ropes, and military equipment.

541. Petrochemicals – Gasoline and petroleum-derived products have powered the energy and transportation industries since the Industrial Revolution.

542. Chlorine – Introduced as a disinfectant in the 19th century, chlorine improved drinking water quality and reduced the spread of diseases.

543. Plastics – Early plastics like Bakelite spurred technological advancements but also created significant environmental challenges.

544. Aluminum – Lightweight and durable, aluminum became essential in aerospace, packaging, and many other industries.

545. Nitrates and synthetic fertilizers – The Haber-Bosch process, developed in 1909, enabled mass fertilizer production, boosting global food supply.

546. CFCs (Freons) – Widely used in refrigerators and air conditioners from the 1930s, CFCs improved living standards but were later restricted due to their impact on the ozone layer.

547. Insulin – Discovered in 1921, insulin enabled effective treatment for diabetes, saving millions of lives.

548. Salt (sodium chloride) – For thousands of years, salt has been a vital preservative and seasoning, playing a crucial role in trade and economies.

549. Laundry detergents – The invention of synthetic detergents in the 1930s revolutionized household cleaning by making washing more effective.

550. Synthetic dyes – The first synthetic dye, mauveine, invented in 1856, transformed the textile industry.

551. Ethanol – Alcohol is a key ingredient in beverages and also serves as a solvent, fuel, and antiseptic.

552. Silicone polymers – Used in medical and cosmetic industries, silicones have applications in implants, sealants, and aerospace technologies.

553. Ammonia – Essential for fertilizers, cleaning, and refrigeration, ammonia is one of the most important industrial chemicals.

554. Graphene – This two-dimensional carbon material, discovered in the 21st century, offers extraordinary strength and conductivity, advancing modern electronics.

555. Teflon – Accidentally discovered in 1938, Teflon became indispensable for nonstick coatings and industrial and military applications.

4. Toxicity and Antidotes

556. Arsenic – Known as the "king of poisons," it has been used for centuries as a lethal agent. The antidote for arsenic poisoning is chelating agents like dimercaprol.

557. Mercury – Mercury and its compounds are highly toxic to the nervous system. Chelators such as sodium dimercaptopropane sulfonate (DMPS) are used to treat mercury poisoning.

558. Cyanide – Blocks cellular respiration. Antidotes include hydroxocobalamin (a form of vitamin B12) and sodium nitrite.

559. Carbon monoxide (CO) – Causes poisoning by preventing oxygen transport in the blood. The antidote is hyperbaric oxygen therapy to accelerate CO removal.

560. Ethanol as an antidote – In cases of methanol or ethylene glycol poisoning, ethanol inhibits their conversion into toxic metabolites by alcohol dehydrogenase.

561. Snake venom – Antivenom serums, prepared by immunizing animals with snake venom, are the primary treatment for snake bites.

562. Botulinum toxin – One of the most potent known toxins. Antitoxin immunoglobulins are used to treat botulism poisoning.

563. Aflatoxins – Produced by molds, they are highly carcinogenic. Treatment includes reducing exposure and supporting liver function.

564. Amphetamines and stimulants – Overdose is managed with benzodiazepines and sedatives to control symptoms.

565. Paracetamol (acetaminophen) – Overdose is treated with N-acetylcysteine, which protects the liver from damage.

566. Blue-ringed octopus venom – Contains tetrodotoxin. There is no direct antidote; treatment involves maintaining vital functions.

567. Digitalis glycosides – Poisoning is treated with activated charcoal and digoxin-specific antibodies.

568. Lead poisoning – Treated with chelators like EDTA (ethylenediaminetetraacetic acid) and dimercaptopropane sulfonate.

569. Organophosphate pesticide poisoning – Treated with atropine and pralidoxime to counteract the effects of the pesticides.

570. Mushroom poisoning (e.g., death cap mushrooms) – Treated with silibinin, derived from milk thistle, to protect the liver.

571. Cisplatin – A chemotherapy drug toxic to the kidneys; treatment includes hydration and protective agents like amifostine.

572. Heavy metals (e.g., cadmium, chromium) – Chelators like dimercaptopropane sulfonate (DMPS) bind heavy metals for removal from the body.

573. Nicotine – Overdose is managed with supportive care, including respiratory support and heart monitoring.

574. Isopropyl alcohol poisoning – Treated with hydration and, in severe cases, dialysis.

575. Fugu fish venom (tetrodotoxin) – Treatment includes intensive medical care and respiratory support, as no specific antidote exists.

5. Surprising Facts About Polymers and Plastics

576. Natural polymers – The first polymers used by humans were natural substances like rubber, wool, and silk, which are the basis for many modern materials.

577. Celluloid – One of the first synthetic polymers, invented in the 19th century, was used to make photographic film, billiard balls, and combs.

578. Polyethylene – The most widely produced plastic in the world, used in packaging, bottles, and food wraps.

579. Polycarbonates – Durable and transparent, they are used in CDs, DVDs, and optical industries.

580. Elastomers – Highly elastic polymers like synthetic rubber are used in tires and seals.

581. Biodegradable polymers – Polylactic acid (PLA), made from corn or sugarcane, is biodegradable and used in eco-friendly packaging.

582. Nylon – Invented in 1935, it was the first synthetic fiber, revolutionizing the textile and military industries, such as for parachutes.

583. Kevlar – A strong polymer used in bulletproof vests, it is five times stronger than steel of the same weight.

584. Polymers in medicine – Many implants, prosthetics, and surgical sutures are made from biocompatible and durable polymers.

585. Teflon – A super-smooth polymer accidentally discovered in 1938, used in nonstick cookware and space technology.

586. Plastic recycling – Not all polymers are easily recyclable, posing environmental challenges, but advances in chemical recycling are emerging.

587. Conductive polymers – Certain polymers, like poly(3,4-ethylenedioxythiophene) (PEDOT), conduct electricity and are used in electronic devices.

588. PMMA (acrylic) – A transparent, lightweight polymer often used as a glass substitute in airplane windows and aquariums.

589. Polyurethane foam – Used in mattresses, insulation, and packaging, it forms through a chemical reaction that creates gas bubbles in the polymer structure.

590. Plastics in space – Polymers like polytetrafluoroethylene (PTFE) are used in space technology for their resistance to extreme temperatures.

591. Thermoplastic polymers – Materials like PET can be melted and reshaped multiple times, commonly used in bottles and packaging.

592. Self-cleaning polymers – Plastics with nanostructures that repel water and dirt are used in car coatings and clothing.

593. Nanopolymers – Applied in nanotechnology, these materials offer exceptional properties like scratch resistance and thermal conductivity.

594. Microplastic problem – The breakdown of larger polymers into microscopic particles poses serious environmental and health risks.

Chapter 7: Time and Space

1. The History of Time and the Calendar

595. The first calendars – The earliest known calendars were lunar, based on the Moon's cycles, and appeared over 10,000 years ago in prehistoric societies.

596. Egyptian calendar – The Egyptians developed a solar calendar around 3000 BCE, based on the rising of the star Sirius and the annual flooding of the Nile.

597. Stonehenge as a clock – Stonehenge in England may have served as a primitive astronomical clock, marking solstices and equinoxes.

598. Mayan calendar – Renowned for its precision, it consisted of the Tzolkin (260 days) and Haab (365 days) cycles, which aligned in a 52-year period.

599. Roman calendar – The original Roman calendar had 10 months. January and February were later added, but the year's 355 days required frequent adjustments.

600. Julian calendar – Introduced by Julius Caesar in 45 BCE, it featured a year length of 365.25 days with a leap day added every four years.

601. Gregorian calendar – Pope Gregory XIII reformed the Julian calendar in 1582, introducing more accurate rules to better align the calendar year with the astronomical year.

602. Sundial – First used in ancient Egypt around 1500 BCE, sundials measured time based on the shadow cast by a gnomon.

603. Clepsydra – Water clocks, or clepsydras, were used in ancient Egypt and Mesopotamia to measure time by the flow of water.

604. Mechanical clock – The first mechanical clocks appeared in 13th-century Europe, primarily in churches to mark prayer hours.

605. Greenwich Mean Time (GMT) – In 1884, an international conference established the Prime Meridian at Greenwich as the reference point for global time measurement.

606. Time zones – Railroads introduced the first time zones in the 19th century to standardize local times across geographically vast countries.

607. Wristwatch revolution – Wristwatches gained popularity in the early 20th century, especially among soldiers during World War I.

608. Atomic timekeeping – The first atomic clock, based on cesium atom vibrations, was built in 1949, offering unparalleled precision.

609. Second as a unit – Since 1967, the second has been defined as 9,192,631,770 periods of radiation corresponding to the cesium-133 atom's transition.

610. Coordinated Universal Time (UTC) – Introduced in 1972, UTC replaced GMT as the global timekeeping standard.

611. Chinese calendar – One of the oldest lunisolar calendars, it is still used to determine traditional holidays such as Chinese New Year.

612. French Republican Calendar – Introduced during the French Revolution in 1793, it featured a 10-day week but was soon abandoned.

613. Time as a relative concept – Einstein's 20th-century theory of relativity transformed our understanding of time, showing it to be dependent on speed and gravitational fields

2. Dimensions and Their Interpretation

614. First dimension – A straight line with only one measurement: length. It forms the basis of geometry, representing the simplest type of space.

615. Second dimension – A plane with two measurements: length and width. It is used in maps, drawings, and images to represent objects.

616. Third dimension – Adds depth to length and width, creating a three-dimensional space, which is the reality we live in and experience.

617. Fourth dimension – According to Einstein's theory of relativity, time is the fourth dimension, combining with three spatial dimensions to form spacetime.

618. Five-dimensional theories – Some physical models, like the Kaluza-Klein theory, propose a fifth dimension to explain electromagnetic phenomena.

619. Dimensions in string theory – String theory posits the existence of up to 10 or 11 dimensions, most of which are "curled up" and inaccessible to observation.

620. Hypercubes (fourth spatial dimension) – In four-dimensional space, objects like the tesseract exist, which is the equivalent of a cube in three dimensions.

621. Minkowski space – Describes spacetime in special relativity, merging spatial and temporal dimensions into a unified framework.

622. Fractals as "fractional dimensions" – Mathematical objects like fractals have non-integer dimensions, indicating a complexity greater than classical dimensions.

623. Perspective in art – Drawings and paintings use principles of perspective to simulate the third dimension on a two-dimensional surface.

624. Gravity and dimensions – Models like the cosmic brane suggest that gravity may "leak" into additional dimensions, explaining its relative weakness in three-dimensional space.

625. Black holes and dimensions – Near black holes, time and space are warped, hinting at the possible existence of extra dimensions within their depths.

626. Dimensions in quantum physics – The "many-worlds" interpretation of quantum mechanics posits that every possible outcome of an experiment exists in a separate dimension.

627. Multiverse – The concept of the multiverse suggests that infinite dimensions and universes may exist, each with its own set of physical laws.

628. N-dimensional geometry – In mathematics, it is possible to describe spaces with any number of dimensions, though visualizing them is challenging for humans.

629. Hilbert space – In quantum mechanics, wave functions exist in Hilbert space, which can have an infinite number of dimensions.

630. Curled-up dimensions – In string theory, extra dimensions are compacted into microscopic scales, making them inaccessible to everyday experience.

631. Time as a flexible dimension – Experiments have shown that time flows more slowly in strong gravitational fields or at high speeds, confirming its dimensional nature.

632. Symmetry and dimensions – Multidimensional symmetry theories, such as supersymmetry, propose the existence of partners for known particles in additional dimensions.

3. Time Travel – Science or Fiction?

633. Einstein's Theory of Relativity—General and special relativity suggest that time is not constant and can be curved by mass and velocity, forming the theoretical foundation for time travel.

634. Time Dilation—Time moves more slowly for objects traveling at speeds close to the speed of light. Astronauts traveling at such speeds could "leap" into the future relative to Earth.

635. Event Horizon of Black Holes—Near a black hole, time slows significantly; theoretically, this could act as a "natural time machine."

636. Wormholes (Spacetime Tunnels)—The theory predicts tunnels connecting different points in spacetime, potentially enabling travel between different times.

637. Grandfather Paradox—A key issue with time travel is the paradox where traveling back in time and altering the past could negate the traveler's existence.

638. Kip Thorne and Time Travel—Physicist Kip Thorne proposed theoretical models for time travel using wormholes, though their stability remains questionable.

639. Time and Multiverses—The many-worlds interpretation suggests that each instance of time travel could create a new timeline, avoiding paradoxes.

640. Experiments with Atomic Clocks—Studies have shown that time moves slower on rapidly moving objects, confirming relativity.

641. Tipler's Time Machine—Mathematical models based on rapidly spinning cylinders suggest they could warp spacetime, allowing time travel.

642. Time as a Dimension—Modern physics treats time as the fourth dimension, opening theoretical possibilities for manipulation, though still unproven.

643. Arrow of Time—According to thermodynamics, time flows in one direction due to increasing entropy, presenting a barrier to traveling to the past.

644. Negative Energy—Time travel, such as through wormholes, would require exotic forms of energy like negative energy, whose existence is uncertain.

645. Criticism of Time Travel—Stephen Hawking argued that paradoxes and the lack of evidence for time travelers suggest that traveling to the past is impossible.

646. Future Time Travel—Theoretically possible through time dilation; an astronaut traveling near the speed of light could return to Earth in the "future."

647. Science Fiction and Science—Stories like H.G. Wells's The Time Machine and movies like Interstellar inspire scientific exploration of time travel, though they remain fictional.

648. Cauchy Horizons—Hypothetical constructs in general relativity could act as time passageways but require conditions impossible in the known universe.

649. LHC and Particles in Time—The Large Hadron Collider (LHC) studies subatomic particles but has found no evidence for time travel.

650. Future Technologies—Advanced civilizations, if they exist, could theoretically develop technologies to manipulate time, but this remains speculative.

651. Quantum Approach—In quantum mechanics, particle states can be entangled in ways that allow "backward" information transfer, but this does not apply to macroscopic objects.

4.Gravity and Its Mysteries

652. Newton's Law of Universal Gravitation—Isaac Newton described gravity as the attractive force between masses, proportional to their product and inversely proportional to the square of the distance between them.

653. Einstein's Theory of Relativity—Albert Einstein revolutionized our understanding of gravity by describing it as the curvature of spacetime caused by mass and energy.

654. Gravity is the Weakest Force—Compared to the other fundamental forces (strong, weak, and electromagnetic), gravity is extraordinarily weak but acts over infinite distances.

655. Gravity and Light—Gravity can bend the path of light, leading to gravitational lensing, an effect observed in astronomy.

656. Gravity and Time—In strong gravitational fields, time flows more slowly, as confirmed by experiments with atomic clocks at different altitudes.

657. Gravitational Waves—Predicted by Einstein in 1916, they were first detected in 2015. These ripples in spacetime are caused by massive events like black hole collisions.

658. Black Holes—Extreme objects where gravity is so intense that nothing, not even light, can escape their event horizons.

659. Gravity and Planet Formation—Gravity causes gas and dust in protoplanetary disks to clump together, forming planets and stars.

660. Microgravity—The weightlessness experienced on the International Space Station results from continuous free-fall in orbit around Earth.

661. Gravity on the Moon—It is about six times weaker than on Earth, allowing astronauts to move and jump more easily.

662. Gravity's Uniformity—Earth's gravity is not uniform; variations in the crust's mass cause local fluctuations in the gravitational field.

663. Dark Matter and Gravity—Invisible matter in the universe is detected only through its gravitational effects on galaxies and light.

664. Gravity and the Universe's Expansion—Dark energy opposes gravity, driving the accelerated expansion of the universe.

665. Gravity and Tidal Forces—The Moon's gravity pulls on Earth, causing tides. Tidal forces also shape planets and moons.

666. Gravity on the Sun—The Sun's gravity keeps planets in orbit while enabling nuclear reactions in its core.

667. Antigravity—Frequently depicted in fiction, there is no scientific evidence for its existence, though dark energy suggests phenomena counteracting gravity.

668. Gravity and Bose-Einstein Condensates—At extremely low temperatures, matter behaves quantum mechanically, influencing its interaction with gravity.

669. Underground Gravity Studies—Experiments like torsion pendulums investigate tiny changes in gravity and seek new particles, such as axions.

670. Gravity and Multidimensional Theories—Some theories suggest gravity "leaks" into extra dimensions, potentially explaining its relative weakness compared to other forces.

671. Gravity in Everyday Life—It underpins systems like GPS, which must account for relativistic effects to ensure accurate measurements.

5.Planetary Motion and Cosmic Harmony

672. Kepler's Laws—Johannes Kepler formulated three laws of planetary motion: orbits are elliptical, planetary velocity varies with distance from the Sun, and orbital period depends on orbit size.

673. Elliptical Orbits—Planetary orbits are ellipses, not perfect circles, with the Sun positioned at one focal point.

674. Gravity as the Driving Force—The Sun's gravitational pull keeps planets on their orbits, preventing them from drifting into space.

675. Orbital Velocity—Earth travels around the Sun at about 107,000 km/h (30 km/s).

676. Planetary Rotation—All planets rotate on their axes, causing day and night cycles.

677. Retrograde Motion—Planets like Venus rotate in a direction opposite to their orbital motion around the Sun, called retrograde rotation.

678. Axial Precession—Earth's axis slowly shifts in a 26,000-year cycle, altering the apparent position of stars over time.

679. Moon Orbits—Moons orbit their planets in elliptical paths, influenced by the gravitational pull of their host planets.

680. Orbital Resonance—Certain celestial bodies, like Jupiter's moons Ganymede, Europa, and Io, have synchronized orbits affecting their dynamics.

681. Harmony of the Spheres—Ancient philosophers like Pythagoras believed planetary movements produced a cosmic "music," known as the harmony of the spheres.

682. The Jupiter Effect—As the largest planet, Jupiter acts as a "shield," diverting comets and asteroids that might threaten Earth.

683. Asteroid Belt—Between Mars and Jupiter lies the asteroid belt, remnants of early solar system formation.

684. Eccentric Orbits—Some exoplanets have highly eccentric orbits, leading to significant variations in their distance from their star.

685. Axial Tilt—Earth's 23.5° axial tilt relative to its orbital plane causes seasonal changes.

686. Years on Other Planets—Orbital periods differ for each planet: Mercury's year lasts 88 Earth days, while Neptune's takes 165 Earth years.

687. Gravitational Tugs—Planets exert gravitational forces on one another, causing slight orbital shifts known as perturbations.

688. Cosmic Catastrophes—Orbital disturbances can lead to events like planets being ejected from their star systems.

689. The Habitable Zone—Planets within the "Goldilocks zone" of their star can maintain liquid water, critical for life.

690. Exoplanetary Systems—Missions like Kepler have discovered thousands of exoplanets, revealing diverse planetary systems in the galaxy.

691. Gravitational Balance—Cosmic harmony stems from the delicate gravitational equilibrium between celestial bodies, ensuring stability over billions of years.

Chapter 8: Mysteries of the Human Mind

1. How Does the Brain Work?

712. The human brain weighs about 1.4 kg—Despite accounting for only 2% of body weight, it consumes around 20% of the body's energy, primarily for processing information and maintaining vital functions.

713. Neurons—The brain contains approximately 86 billion neurons that communicate through chemical and electrical signals across synapses.

714. Nerve impulse transmission—Nerve impulses in neurons can travel up to 120 m/s, enabling rapid information processing.

715. Cerebral cortex—This outer brain layer is responsible for higher functions such as thinking, planning, language, and consciousness.

716. Brain hemispheres—The left hemisphere is often associated with logic and language, while the right is linked to creativity and intuition, though both work in concert.

717. Hippocampus—This brain region is crucial for long-term memory and spatial navigation.

718. Limbic system—Includes brain areas linked to emotions, memory, and behavior, such as the amygdala and hippocampus.

719. Brain plasticity—The brain can change its structure and functions in response to learning and experiences, even in adulthood.

720. Neurotransmitters—Chemicals like dopamine, serotonin, and acetylcholine relay signals between neurons, influencing mood, memory, and cognition.

721. Brain and sleep—During sleep, the brain processes memories, regenerates, and clears toxic waste through the glymphatic system.

722. Cerebral blood flow—The brain is highly vascularized, with about 750 ml of blood flowing through it per minute to supply oxygen and glucose.

723. Role of the cerebellum—Located at the back of the brain, the cerebellum coordinates movement, balance, and precision.

724. Visual cortex—Located in the occipital lobe, it processes visual information, enabling recognition of shapes, colors, and motion.

725. Language processing—The Broca's and Wernicke's areas in the brain are responsible for speech production and comprehension, respectively. Damage can lead to aphasia.

726. Mirror neuron effect—Mirror neurons activate both when performing actions and observing others, facilitating empathy and learning through imitation.

727. Hormones in the brain—Hormones like oxytocin and cortisol influence mood, stress, and social behaviors.

728. Headaches—Headaches often stem from tension in muscles or blood vessels around the brain, as the brain itself lacks pain receptors.

729. Electrical signals—EEG (electroencephalography) measures brain electrical activity, helping study sleep, seizures, and other brain functions.

730. Hypoxia and the brain—The brain is highly sensitive to oxygen deprivation; irreversible damage occurs within minutes without oxygen.

731. Brain development—While the brain evolves throughout life, its growth is most rapid in childhood, with numerous synaptic connections forming at that stage.

2. Senses – Our Tools of Perception

732. Five primary senses—Traditionally, sight, hearing, smell, taste, and touch are recognized as the main senses, enabling us to perceive and interpret the external world.

733. Vision—The eye captures light, focusing it on the retina where photoreceptors (cones and rods) convert it into electrical signals transmitted to the brain.

734. Hearing—The ear converts sound waves into mechanical vibrations, which are then processed into electrical impulses by the cochlea in the inner ear.

735. Smell—Receptor cells in the nose detect odor molecules, sending signals to the olfactory bulb, which analyzes the scents.

736. Taste—Taste buds on the tongue identify five primary flavors: sweet, sour, salty, bitter, and umami (savory).

737. Touch—Skin receptors respond to pressure, vibration, temperature, and pain, transmitting information to the brain via the nervous system.

738. Proprioception—Known as the "sixth sense," it enables body orientation in space through receptors in muscles, tendons, and joints.

739. Sense of balance—The vestibular system in the inner ear detects head position and body movement to maintain equilibrium.

740. Sensory adaptation—Our senses can adjust to constant stimuli; for example, we stop noticing a persistent smell after prolonged exposure.

741. Sensory illusions—The senses can deceive us, such as with optical illusions where the brain misinterprets visual information.

742. Sense of pain (nociception)—Special receptors in the skin and internal organs detect tissue damage and send pain signals to the brain.

743. Color sensitivity—The human eye distinguishes millions of shades through three types of cones sensitive to red, green, and blue light.

744. Smell and memory—The sense of smell is closely tied to the limbic system, making it uniquely powerful in evoking memories and emotions.

745. Role of the tongue in taste—The tongue has regions slightly more sensitive to certain tastes, but all taste buds can detect all types of flavors.

746. Emotional touch—Special nerve fibers in the skin respond to gentle touch, playing a role in building social bonds.

747. Hearing ultrasounds—Although humans cannot perceive ultrasounds, some mammals, such as bats, use them for echolocation.

748. Synesthesia—Some individuals experience a "blending" of senses, such as seeing sounds as colors or associating tastes with shapes.

749. Phantom sensations—After limb amputation, patients may feel "phantom" pain or sensations as though the limb still exists.

750. Animal senses—Some animals have extraordinary senses; for example, sharks detect electric fields, and migratory birds use Earth's magnetic field for navigation.

751. Technology and senses—Devices like artificial retinas and cochlear implants help individuals with impaired vision or hearing regain sensory functions.

3. Dreams and Their Significance

752. What are dreams?—Dreams are sequences of images, sounds, and emotions occurring in the mind during sleep, primarily in the REM (Rapid Eye Movement) phase.

753. REM phase—Most dreams occur during REM sleep, when brain activity resembles wakefulness, but the body's muscles are relaxed.

754. Everyone dreams—Even those who claim not to dream likely do but fail to remember their dreams.

755. Symbolism in dreams—Dreams often include symbols and metaphors that may relate to emotions, memories, or hidden thoughts.

756. Freud on dreams—Sigmund Freud considered dreams "the royal road to the unconscious," reflecting hidden desires and fears.

757. Jung and archetypes—Carl Gustav Jung viewed dreams as a path to the collective unconscious, full of archetypes and universal symbols.

758. Emotional processing function—Dreams may help the brain process intense emotions and cope with challenging experiences.

759. Role of dreams in memory—Studies suggest that dreams support memory consolidation, organizing information gathered during the day.

760. Nightmares—Often linked to stress or trauma, nightmares might be the brain's way of processing difficult emotions.

761. Sleep paralysis—This condition occurs when a person wakes up but cannot move, often accompanied by intense fear and "sleep hallucinations."

762. Lucid dreaming—In lucid dreams, the dreamer becomes aware they are dreaming and can partially control the dream's content.

763. Déjà vu and dreams—Some researchers propose that the feeling of déjà vu might stem from unconsciously remembered dreams.

764. Dreams and mental health—Irregular dreams or their absence can be associated with mental health issues such as depression or PTSD.

765. Colors in dreams—Most people dream in color, although some report black-and-white dreams, which may depend on lifestyle and visual experiences.

766. Animals also dream—EEG studies show that many animals, including dogs and cats, experience REM sleep and likely dream.

767. Prophetic dreams—Some people claim their dreams predicted future events, though science attributes this to coincidental correlations.

768. Sleep amnesia—Most dreams are forgotten within minutes of waking because the brain does not prioritize them as significant memories.

769. Flying dreams—Often interpreted as a reflection of freedom or a desire to break free from constraints.

770. Dreams and culture—Dreams hold varying meanings across cultures; in some beliefs, they are seen as messages from gods or spirits.

771. Research on dreams—Scientists use technologies like fMRI to study brain activity during sleep and attempt to "read" dream content.

4. Neurobiology of Emotions

772. What are emotions?—Emotions are complex responses of the brain and body to external or internal stimuli, influencing thoughts, behaviors, and physiological reactions.

773. Limbic system—The primary center for processing emotions in the brain, including structures like the amygdala, hippocampus, and hypothalamus.

774. Amygdala—Responsible for recognizing and processing emotions, especially fear and aggression, and for triggering threat responses.

775. Prefrontal cortex—Regulates emotions, controls impulses, and helps make decisions based on emotional experiences.

776. Neurotransmitters and emotions—Chemicals like dopamine, serotonin, and norepinephrine influence mood and the ability to experience pleasure.

777. Oxytocin—Often called the "love hormone," it plays a crucial role in forming social bonds, empathy, and trust.

778. Cortisol—Known as the "stress hormone," it is released in threatening situations and affects the body's and mind's response to stress.

779. Dopamine and reward—Dopamine is central to the brain's reward system, motivating repeated behaviors that bring pleasure.

780. Serotonin and mood—Low levels of serotonin are linked to depression, anxiety, and other mood disorders.

781. Structures tied to happiness—Activity in areas like the nucleus accumbens and prefrontal cortex is associated with feelings of happiness and satisfaction.

782. Fear and the amygdala—The amygdala quickly evaluates stimuli as potentially dangerous, triggering a "fight or flight" response.

783. Empathy and mirror neurons—These neurons activate both when experiencing emotions and observing them in others, supporting empathetic abilities.

784. Emotions and memory—Strong emotions enhance memory processes, making events tied to intense feelings easier to recall.

785. Hypothalamus and stress—The hypothalamus activates the HPA axis (hypothalamus-pituitary-adrenal), regulating the body's stress responses.

786. Depression and neurochemistry—Imbalances in serotonin, dopamine, and norepinephrine levels can contribute to depression.

787. Role of endorphins—Called "natural opiates," endorphins alleviate pain and produce euphoria, such as after physical exercise.

788. Emotions and health—Chronic stress and negative emotions can weaken the immune system, increasing the risk of illnesses.

789. Joy and brain activity—Studies show joy is associated with heightened activity in the left hemisphere of the brain, particularly in the prefrontal area.

790. Anxiety and anxiety disorders—Excessive amygdala activity and insufficient prefrontal control can result in anxiety states.

791. Emotional plasticity—The brain can adapt emotional responses through experiences, therapy, and practices like meditation or mindfulness.

5.Cognitive Abilities and Their Limits

792. Cognitive abilities—Include processes such as thinking, memory, attention, perception, problem-solving, language, and decision-making.

793. Working memory—The ability to hold and manipulate information for a short period; its capacity averages 7±2 items.

794. Long-term memory—The brain can store vast amounts of information in long-term memory throughout a lifetime, though retrieval depends on repetition and associations.

795. Limits of attention—Humans can consciously focus on one or at most two tasks simultaneously; multitasking reduces efficiency.

796. Stroop effect—Demonstrates attention processing limits when the color of a word conflicts with its meaning, slowing responses.

797. Cognitive heuristics—The mind uses simplified strategies ("rules of thumb") that are quick but may lead to cognitive biases.

798. Confirmation bias—People tend to seek information that supports their beliefs while ignoring contradictory evidence.

799. Analysis paralysis—Excessive information or choices can make decision-making difficult, a phenomenon known as "paralysis by analysis."

800. Limits of perception—Human senses have restricted ranges, e.g., vision only detects light wavelengths between 400–700 nm, and hearing ranges from 20–20,000 Hz.

801. Dunning-Kruger effect—Individuals with low competence in a field tend to overestimate their knowledge.

802. Neuroplasticity—Despite limits, the brain can adapt and develop new abilities in response to learning and experiences.

803. Processing speed—The brain processes information in about 120 ms, enabling rapid reactions but causing slight delays in perceiving reality.

804. Episodic memory and false memories—Episodic memory is prone to errors; people can create false memories due to suggestions.

805. Limits of logical thinking—Emotions and biases can affect the ability to reason logically, even when faced with facts.

806. Problem-solving boundaries—The human mind excels at solving concrete-visual problems but struggles with abstract ones.

807. Cognitive automation—Once a skill is mastered, like driving, many processes become automatic, reducing the load on working memory.

808. Prediction limits—The brain predicts future events based on experiences and models, which can sometimes lead to incorrect conclusions.

809. Learning constraints—Learning speed and capacity decrease with age, although new technologies and techniques can slow this decline.

810. Challenges for AI—The human brain still surpasses artificial intelligence in creativity, empathy, and adaptability to new situations.

811. Creativity and intuition—Considered among the hardest cognitive abilities to explain and replicate, as they rely on unconscious brain processes.

Chapter 9: Evolution and the History of Life

1.The Origins of Life on Earth

812. Primordial Earth—Around 4.5 billion years ago, Earth was a hot ball of magma that gradually cooled, forming a crust and an atmosphere rich in carbon dioxide, methane, and ammonia.

813. Formation of oceans—Condensation of water vapor released by volcanoes around 4 billion years ago created primordial oceans, which became the cradle of life.

814. Abiogenesis theory—Proposes that life originated from non-living chemical compounds, energized by factors such as UV radiation and electrical discharges, forming the first organic molecules.

815. Miller-Urey experiment (1953)—Scientists demonstrated that amino acids, the building blocks of proteins, could be synthesized under conditions resembling Earth's early atmosphere.

816. First organic compounds—Likely formed in warm pools where simple carbon-based molecules interacted, creating more complex structures.

817. Role of clay—Clay might have acted as a catalyst, aiding the organization of organic molecules into larger structures like RNA.

818. RNA world hypothesis—Suggests that early life was based on RNA, which could store genetic information and catalyze chemical reactions.

819. First cells—Around 3.8 billion years ago, protocells with lipid membranes emerged, enabling the preservation and exchange of substances.

820. Archaea—Ancient microorganisms resembling modern archaea may have been the first life forms capable of surviving extreme conditions.

821. Anaerobic photosynthesis—Early photosynthetic organisms, such as green sulfur bacteria, used hydrogen sulfide instead of water as an electron source.

822. Oxygen emergence—Around 2.5 billion years ago, cyanobacteria began oxygenic photosynthesis, releasing oxygen into the atmosphere and triggering the Great Oxygenation Event.

823. Great Oxygenation Event—The rise of atmospheric oxygen around 2.4 billion years ago revolutionized life on Earth, allowing aerobic organisms to thrive.

824. First eukaryotes—Emerged around 1.8 billion years ago through endosymbiosis, where one cell engulfed another, forming structures like mitochondria.

825. Hydrothermal hypothesis—Proposes that life originated in deep ocean hydrothermal vents, rich in energy and chemical compounds.

826. Stromatolite fossils—The oldest known fossils, dating back 3.5 billion years, are from cyanobacteria that formed stromatolites in shallow waters.

827. Evolution of metabolism—Early life forms relied on fermentation and chemosynthesis before developing more efficient processes like aerobic respiration.

828. Lithosphere and life—Microorganisms may have survived in rock crevices, protected from UV radiation and temperature extremes.

829. Panspermia—Suggests life could have arrived on Earth from space via microorganisms on meteorites.

830. Prebiotic chemistry—Processes on Earth before life emerged likely included the synthesis of essential organic molecules such as nucleotides and amino acids.

831. Beginning of biological evolution—When the first self-replicating RNA or DNA molecules became enclosed in membranes, the era of evolution through natural selection began.

2. Dinosaurs – Facts That Amaze

832. Dinosaurs dominated for 165 million years—They thrived from the Late Triassic (about 230 million years ago) to the end of the Cretaceous (66 million years ago).

833. Not all were giants—Most dinosaurs were the size of modern livestock, with some, like Compsognathus, being as small as a chicken.

834. Dinosaurs had feathers—Many species, especially theropods, were feathered for insulation, communication, or early attempts at flight.

835. Tyrannosaurus rex wasn't the fastest—Its estimated top speed was around 20 km/h (12 mph), making it slower compared to other dinosaurs.

836. Dinosaurs still exist—Modern birds are direct descendants of small, feathered dinosaurs.

837. Largest land dinosaur—Argentinosaurus, a colossal sauropod, could reach up to 35 meters in length and weigh over 70 tons.

838. Smallest dinosaur—Oculudentavis khaungraae, resembling today's hummingbirds, was about 5 cm long.

839. Not all dinosaurs went extinct at once—Some populations may have survived locally for several thousand years after the Cretaceous mass extinction.

840. Dinosaurs had complex brains—Certain species, like Troodon, had relatively large brains compared to their body size, indicating advanced behaviors.

841. Dinosaur teeth were replaceable—Species like ceratopsians could replace their teeth multiple times during their lifetime.

842. Dietary diversity—Dinosaurs ranged from carnivorous (Velociraptor) and herbivorous (Stegosaurus) to omnivorous.

843. Brontosaurus is back—Long considered a misclassification, recent studies have reinstated it as a distinct genus.

844. Dinosaur colors—Pigment analysis of fossilized feathers suggests dinosaurs may have had diverse and vibrant colors.

845. Largest predator—Spinosaurus was larger than Tyrannosaurus, reaching up to 18 meters, and likely lived a semi-aquatic lifestyle.

846. Dinosaurs and continents—Their distribution was shaped by continental drift; during the Triassic, they lived on the supercontinent Pangaea.

847. Dinosaur communication—Some species likely used sounds, gestures, and colors for communication, similar to modern birds and reptiles.

848. Dinosaurs and mass extinction—The asteroid impact 66 million years ago caused a global winter, leading to the extinction of non-avian dinosaurs.

849. Fossilized eggs—Discoveries of dinosaur eggs reveal that many species cared for their young by building nests and tending to them.

850. Dinosaurs and the asteroid—The Chicxulub crater on the Yucatán Peninsula, measuring 150 km wide, marks the asteroid's impact site that contributed to their extinction.

851. Scientific reconstructions—Advanced technologies like CT scans and computer modeling allow scientists to recreate dinosaur appearances and behaviors.

3. Mass Extinctions in Planetary History

852. Five major extinctions—Earth has experienced five major mass extinctions: the Ordovician-Silurian, Devonian, Permian, Triassic, and Cretaceous events.

853. Ordovician-Silurian (445 million years ago)—Approximately 85% of species, mostly marine, perished due to rapid cooling and sea-level decline.

854. Devonian (375 million years ago)—About 75% of species disappeared, likely caused by environmental changes such as oxygen depletion in oceans.

855. Permian (252 million years ago)—The largest extinction event, the "Great Dying," wiped out 96% of marine species and 70% of land species, mainly due to volcanic eruptions and climate shifts.

856. Triassic (201 million years ago)—Around 80% of species vanished, paving the way for dinosaur dominance; causes include volcanic activity and increased CO_2 levels.

857. Cretaceous (66 million years ago)—76% of species, including all non-avian dinosaurs, went extinct following an asteroid impact and subsequent "nuclear winter."

858. Crater evidence—The Chicxulub crater on the Yucatán Peninsula is direct evidence of the asteroid impact that ended the Cretaceous period.

859. Siberian Traps eruptions—Massive volcanic eruptions in Siberia during the Permian extinction released greenhouse gases, triggering global warming.

860. Ocean hypoxia—Some extinctions saw such low oxygen levels in oceans that most marine life could not survive.

861. Glaciations—Global cooling and ice ages caused habitat loss and contributed to certain extinction events.

862. Sea level changes—Fluctuations in sea levels destroyed coastal and marine ecosystems, exacerbating extinction rates.

863. Megafauna extinction—During the Pleistocene (about 10,000 years ago), most large land animals vanished, likely due to climate changes and human activity.

864. Recovery time—Biodiversity took millions of years to recover after mass extinctions; for example, recovery after the Permian extinction took about 10 million years.

865. Regional extinctions—Not all extinctions were global; some were confined to specific regions or groups of species.

866. Global warming and extinctions—Rapid climate changes linked to greenhouse gas emissions were a common factor in many extinction events.

867. Acid rain—Asteroid impacts or volcanic eruptions could cause acid rain, devastating vegetation and food chains.

868. Supernova impacts—Some theories suggest supernova explosions could have altered Earth's atmosphere, damaging the ozone layer and triggering extinctions.

869. Anthropocene: the sixth extinction—The current extinction rate, driven by human activities, is comparable to previous mass extinctions.

870. Lessons from extinctions—Studying past mass extinctions helps predict the effects of modern environmental changes and develop biodiversity conservation strategies.

871. Biodiversity as a buffer—The resilience of ecosystems after extinctions underscores the importance of maintaining diverse species to withstand future changes.

4.The Evolution of Humans

872. Shared ancestor of humans and apes—Humans share a common ancestor with chimpanzees that lived around 6–8 million years ago.

873. Sahelanthropus tchadensis—One of the oldest known human ancestors, it lived approximately 7 million years ago, exhibiting both ape-like and human-like traits.

874. Australopithecus afarensis—Known as "Lucy," this hominid lived about 3.9–2.9 million years ago and demonstrated the ability to walk on two legs.

875. Bipedalism—Walking upright was a critical evolutionary adaptation, allowing long-distance travel and freeing hands for tool use.

876. Homo habilis—Considered the first member of the Homo genus, it lived about 2.4–1.4 million years ago and created simple stone tools.

877. Homo erectus—One of the longest-surviving human species (1.9 million–110,000 years ago), it mastered fire and migrated out of Africa.

878. Neanderthals (Homo neanderthalensis)—Living in Europe and Asia from around 400,000 to 40,000 years ago, they were robust and used advanced tools.

879. Neanderthal culture—Neanderthals created ornaments, buried their dead, and likely had some form of linguistic communication.

880. Homo sapiens—Emerging in Africa around 300,000 years ago, our species is characterized by abstract thinking and advanced cultural creation.

881. Out-of-Africa migration—Homo sapiens left Africa approximately 70,000 years ago, colonizing Europe, Asia, Australia, and the Americas.

882. Genetic interbreeding—Modern humans interbred with Neanderthals and Denisovans, leaving genetic traces in present-day human genomes.

883. Brain development—The Homo sapiens brain reached an average volume of 1350 cm³, facilitating language, tool use, and complex social structures.

884. Fire as a breakthrough—Mastery of fire allowed for cooking food, increasing caloric availability and promoting brain development.

885. Cognitive revolution—Around 70,000 years ago, Homo sapiens began creating abstract concepts, art, and advanced communication, accelerating cultural development.

886. First tools—Humans crafted tools from stone, bone, and wood, which became increasingly sophisticated over time.

887. Neolithic revolution—About 10,000 years ago, Homo sapiens began farming and domesticating animals, leading to the establishment of settled communities.

888. Language—The development of language enabled Homo sapiens to share knowledge, advance culture, and organize into larger societies.

889. Social evolution—Modern humans created complex social hierarchies, religions, and political systems, shaping the rise of civilization.

890. Modern genetics—DNA studies confirm the common origin of all humans from a small African population approximately 200,000 years ago.

891. Future evolution—Factors such as technology, environmental changes, and genetic engineering may shape the continued evolution of humanity.

5.The Genome and Its Mysteries

892. What is a genome?—The genome is the complete set of an organism's genetic material, containing DNA with instructions needed for building and functioning.

893. Size of the human genome—The human genome comprises approximately 3 billion base pairs that encode around 20,000–25,000 genes.

894. DNA as the information carrier—DNA consists of four nitrogenous bases (adenine, thymine, cytosine, guanine), forming the genetic code.

895. Protein-coding genes—Only about 1.5% of human DNA codes for proteins; the rest serves regulatory functions or remains not fully understood.

896. Mitochondrial genome—Mitochondria have their own small genome inherited exclusively from the mother, crucial for cellular energy production.

897. Genome sequencing—The Human Genome Project (1990–2003) enabled the complete reading of the human genome, revolutionizing biology and medicine.

898. Genetic polymorphisms—Differences in DNA sequences between individuals (e.g., SNPs—single nucleotide polymorphisms) affect traits and disease susceptibility.

899. Junk DNA—Once thought to be useless, much of this DNA is now known to have regulatory roles.

900. Epigenome—Includes chemical modifications like DNA methylation, influencing gene activity without altering the sequence.

901. Haplotypes—Groups of genes inherited together provide insights into geographical origins and population history.

902. Genes and diseases—Mutations in DNA can lead to genetic disorders, such as cystic fibrosis, sickle cell anemia, or Down syndrome.

903. CRISPR-Cas9—This cutting-edge genome editing technology allows precise DNA modifications, opening avenues for treating genetic diseases.

904. Human genome compared to others—The human genome shares about 98% similarity with chimpanzees, indicating a shared evolutionary origin.

905. Archaic genome—DNA analysis of Neanderthals and Denisovans reveals that modern humans share 1%–3% of their genes with these archaic humans.

906. Transposons—"Jumping genes" that move within the genome, influencing evolution and genetic functions.

907. Telomeres—Protective "caps" at the ends of chromosomes that shorten with age and are linked to aging and diseases.

908. Genome and adaptation—DNA changes enable organisms to adapt to their environment, e.g., genes for lactose tolerance evolved in humans through animal domestication.

909. Viruses in the genome—Parts of human DNA originate from ancient viruses that integrated their genes into our genome.

910. Personalized medicine—Genomic analysis facilitates tailored therapies, adapted to individual genetic predispositions.

911. The genome of the future—Advances in genetics may enable controlling inherited diseases, extending life, and modifying human traits, raising ethical concerns.

Chapter 10. Unsolved Mysteries of Science

1. Mysterious Natural Phenomena

912. Lights in the sky (ball lightning)—Rare and elusive phenomena, such as glowing spheres observed during storms, remain subjects of scientific debate.

913. Moving rocks in Death Valley—Stones on the dry lakebed in California shift across the surface, leaving tracks, yet their motion isn't fully understood.

914. Hessdalen lights—Mysterious lights in Norway have appeared for decades without an apparent cause, intriguing scientists.

915. Rains of fish and frogs—Reported worldwide, these events are thought to result from storms that lift animals into the atmosphere.

916. Microplastics in rain—Scientists are discovering microplastics in rainfall globally, but their environmental and health impacts remain unclear.

917. The oceanic "bloop" sound—A loud underwater sound recorded in the 1990s has an unknown origin, sparking various theories.

918. Crystal caves—Massive selenite crystals in Mexico's Naica cave puzzle geologists with their formation and implications.

919. Spontaneous human combustion—Rare and controversial reports of people allegedly bursting into flames continue to divide scientific opinion.

920. The Taos hum—A low-frequency hum heard in places like Taos, New Mexico, lacks a known source, fueling theories from acoustic to paranormal.

921. Volcanic lightning—Electrical discharges during volcanic eruptions are observed, but their exact formation mechanisms are unclear.

922. Desert roses—Gypsum crystal formations resembling flowers require precise climatic conditions, sparking interest in their formation.

923. Oceanic mareographs—Unexplained ocean waves, such as those from unknown origins, are studied in relation to earthquakes and underwater eruptions.

924. Strange flashes in space—Events like fast radio bursts (FRBs) recorded by telescopes have an enigmatic origin.

925. Crop circles—While many are man-made, intricate designs raise questions about their creation.

926. Frozen methane bubbles—Seen in lakes in Canada and Siberia, trapped methane creates patterns, raising environmental concerns over greenhouse gas release.

927. Giant ocean eddies—Massive oceanic whirlpools like the Great Pacific Eddy impact global climates, but their dynamics are poorly understood.

928. Auroras—The basic mechanics of auroras (solar particles interacting with Earth's magnetosphere) are known, but their intensity and shapes remain unpredictable.

929. Ghostly fog apparitions—Reports of "ghosts" in misty conditions may result from rare atmospheric and light conditions.

930. Unidentified ocean objects—Rare phenomena like sonar anomalies hint at unknown underwater structures or species.

931. Bright flashes from cosmic sources—Some bursts of energy from deep space defy explanation, suggesting unknown astrophysical processes.

2.Do Other Universes Exist?

932. Multiverse concept—The multiverse theory proposes the existence of multiple universes, each potentially with different physical laws, structures, and histories.

933. String theory—Suggests that 10 or 11 dimensions exist, and different universes may result from various configurations of strings.

934. Cosmic inflation—The hypothesis of eternal inflation posits that our universe is just one of many "bubbles" formed during the expansion of spacetime.

935. Parallel universes—Quantum theory suggests that every event with multiple outcomes leads to a branching of universes, creating parallel realities.

936. "Matryoshka" universes—This hypothesis envisions universes nested within one another, akin to Russian nesting dolls.

937. Universes from black holes—Some scientists speculate that the interiors of black holes could give rise to new universes.

938. Multiverse and physical constants—Different universes may have varying values for constants, such as the speed of light or particle masses, shaping their properties.

939. Observational evidence—Studies of cosmic microwave background radiation hint at possible "collisions" between universes, though evidence remains inconclusive.

940. Quantum coherence—Phenomena like superposition in quantum mechanics may hint at the existence of parallel universes.

941. Universes in holographic theory—Some physicists propose that our universe might be a hologram, with other universes existing in separate "projections."

942. Event horizons—Parallel universes might be separated from us by barriers like event horizons, making direct observation impossible.

943. Brane universes in M-theory—M-theory suggests that universes could be three-dimensional membranes (branes) floating in a higher-dimensional space.

944. Dark energy—The high level of dark energy in our universe suggests that universes with varying amounts of dark energy might also exist.

945. Lifeless universes—If physical constants differ, many universes might be "dead," unable to sustain life.

946. Quantum gravity models—Efforts to unify quantum mechanics and general relativity may provide tools to explore the multiverse.

947. Philosophy of the multiverse—The idea of multiple universes raises philosophical questions about our place in reality and the nature of existence.

948. Thought experiments—Concepts like "Schrödinger's cat" support the idea that all quantum possibilities may exist simultaneously.

949. Limits of observation—Technological constraints on telescopes and scientific instruments make studying other universes speculative.

950. Future theories—Advances in physics, such as quantum gravity and research into dark matter, could one day provide evidence for the multiverse.

951. Scientific skepticism—While intriguing, the multiverse remains a theoretical construct lacking direct experimental evidence.

3. Dark Energy and Dark Matter

952. What is dark matter? – It is an invisible substance that neither emits nor absorbs light but exerts a gravitational influence on the motion of galaxies and galaxy clusters.

953. What is dark energy? – A mysterious form of energy that accelerates the expansion of the universe, counteracting gravity.

954. Proportion in the universe – Dark matter accounts for about 27% of the universe's mass-energy, dark energy 68%, and ordinary matter just 5%.

955. Gravitational lensing effect – Observations of light bending around massive objects indicate the presence of invisible dark matter.

956. Motion of galaxies – The rotation of galaxies does not match the visible amount of matter; additional unseen mass attributed to dark matter is required.

957. Dark matter halos – Galaxies are surrounded by large "halos" of dark matter that stabilize their structure.

958. WIMP particles – Weakly interacting massive particles (WIMPs) are among the leading candidates for the composition of dark matter.

959. Axions – Another hypothetical particle that could form dark matter; their existence is being investigated in laboratories worldwide.

960. Expansion of the universe – The discovery of the universe's accelerating expansion in the 1990s pointed to the existence of dark energy.

961. Cosmological constant – Dark energy is sometimes identified with Einstein's cosmological constant, representing vacuum energy.

962. Quintessence – An alternative theory suggests dark energy is a dynamic field that changes over time.

963. Nature of dark matter – It is unknown whether dark matter consists of elementary particles or has entirely different, unknown properties.

964. Earth-based experiments – Detectors such as Xenon1T attempt to directly detect dark matter particles but have yet to succeed.

965. Cosmic observations – Telescopes like Hubble and James Webb contribute to studying the effects of dark matter and dark energy on distant objects.

966. Dwarf galaxies – Analyses suggest that dwarf galaxies may contain more dark matter than visible matter.

967. CMB (Cosmic Microwave Background) – Fluctuations in the CMB provide evidence of dark matter and dark energy's presence in the early universe.

968. MOND hypothesis – Modified Newtonian Dynamics (MOND) tries to explain effects attributed to dark matter without requiring an invisible substance.

969. Impact on the universe's future – The dominance of dark energy suggests the universe will continue its accelerated expansion, possibly leading to a "cold death."

970. A grand scientific challenge – Both dark energy and dark matter remain among the greatest unsolved mysteries of modern physics, requiring new physics beyond the standard model.

4. Extraterrestrial Intelligence – Evidence and Hypotheses

972. Drake Equation – A formula developed by Frank Drake to estimate the number of technological civilizations in our galaxy based on several factors.

973. SETI Project – The Search for Extraterrestrial Intelligence is a global effort to listen for radio signals from space that could originate from alien civilizations.

974. Wow! Signal – In 1977, a mysterious 72-second radio signal was detected and has never been explained, but it is considered a potential extraterrestrial contact.

975. Exoplanets – Missions like Kepler have discovered thousands of planets outside the Solar System, many of which are in the habitable zone suitable for life.

976. Mars – Studies of Mars have revealed evidence of ancient rivers and lakes, suggesting the possibility of microbial life in the past.

977. Europa and Enceladus – The icy moons of Jupiter and Saturn may harbor subsurface oceans of liquid water, potentially conducive to life.

978. Panspermia Hypothesis – Proposes that life may have originated elsewhere in the cosmos and was brought to Earth via meteorites.

979. Astrobiology – The field studying life in extreme conditions on Earth, suggesting similar organisms could exist beyond our planet.

980. 'Oumuamua – This mysterious interstellar object passed through the Solar System in 2017, sparking speculation about a possible artificial origin.

981. Signs on Venus? – In 2020, the discovery of phosphine in Venus' atmosphere suggested the potential for microbial life in its upper atmospheric layers.

982. Fermi Paradox – If intelligent life is common, we should have detected it by now; the lack of evidence raises the question: "Where is everyone?"

983. Technosignatures – The search for advanced technology, such as megastructures (e.g., Dyson spheres), that could indicate the presence of intelligent civilizations.

984. Kardashev Scale – Describes civilizations capable of harnessing energy from their planet (Type I), star (Type II), or galaxy (Type III).

985. Close Encounters – Reports of UFO sightings, while controversial, are analyzed for potential signs of contact with intelligent beings.

986. Microbial Life Beyond Earth – Searching for evidence of microorganisms in samples from Mars, Europa, or comets remains a scientific priority.

987. Shadow Biosphere Hypothesis – Suggests life on Earth may have developed parallel "shadow" forms that are difficult to detect with current methods.

988. Tabby's Star Observations – Irregular brightness changes in this star were speculated to result from artificial megastructures, though no conclusive evidence has been found.

989. Life in Gas Giants' Atmospheres – The atmospheres of Jupiter or Saturn could have layers with conditions favorable to simple forms of life.

990. Evolutionary Filter – A theory proposing that there may be barriers most civilizations fail to overcome, explaining the lack of contact with extraterrestrial intelligence.

5. Future of Science – Unanswered Questions

992. What is consciousness? – The question of what consciousness is and how it arises in the brain remains one of modern science's greatest challenges.

993. Can we travel through time? – Theoretical foundations for time travel exist within general relativity, but practical realization remains unknown.

994. What came before the Big Bang? – The question of the universe's beginning and what might have existed before the Big Bang is among the hardest to solve.

995. What are dark energy and dark matter? – These mysterious components of the universe, comprising over 95% of its mass-energy, are not yet fully understood.

996. How did life originate? – The exact mechanisms of abiogenesis, the process by which life arose from non-living matter, remain elusive.

997. Is the universe infinite? – The nature of the universe—whether it is infinite or finite in size—remains an open question.

998. Do other universes exist? – The multiverse hypothesis suggests our universe is one of many, but direct evidence is lacking for verification.

999. Can quantum mechanics and general relativity be unified? – Developing a quantum theory of gravity to reconcile these two fundamental frameworks is one of physics' greatest challenges.

1000. Will artificial intelligence achieve self-awareness? – The development of AI raises questions about whether machines capable of independent thought and emotions can be created.

1001. Are we alone in the universe? – The possibility of intelligent life beyond Earth remains one of the most fascinating questions in science.

1002. Can an infinite energy source be created? – Technologies like fusion reactors, which could provide virtually unlimited energy, are still under development.

1003. How can entropy be reversed? – The second law of thermodynamics predicts inevitable increases in entropy; whether this process can be reversed is an open question.

1004. Is time fundamental? – Some physicists suggest that time may be an illusion or an emergent property of deeper processes, raising questions about its true nature.

1005. How far can we travel into space? – The potential for interstellar travel is currently constrained by technological limits and the speed of light.

1006. Can aging be prevented? – Research on genetics, telomeres, and stem cells offers potential for life extension, but its ultimate limits remain unknown.

1007. What are the limits of human perception? – Our senses and technology allow us to perceive only a fraction of reality; are there phenomena beyond our reach?

1008. Will we fully understand the brain? – Despite advances in neuroscience, achieving a complete understanding of the human brain remains distant.

1009. Are the laws of physics universal? – Some speculate that the laws of physics might vary in different regions of the universe or other dimensions.

1010. What is humanity's future? – From colonizing other planets to developing transhumanist technologies, the future of humanity is one of the greatest uncertainties.

6. Barriers and Breakthroughs in Science

1012. Speed of Light Barriers—According to relativity, the speed of light is an unbreakable limit, but the hypothetical existence of tachyons suggests it might be possible to surpass it.

1013. Black Holes and Information—The information paradox in black holes remains unsolved; what happens to information when matter falls into a black hole?

1014. Breakthroughs in Nanotechnology—While nanotechnology promises revolutionary advances in medicine, energy, and materials, questions about its limitations and ethical consequences remain.

1015. Interstellar Hibernation—Research continues into the possibility of placing humans into hibernation for long-duration space travel.

1016. Future of Climate—Science predicts rising Earth temperatures, but effective strategies to curb emissions and prevent catastrophic changes are still unclear.

1017. Supersymmetric Particles—Experiments like the LHC are still searching for supersymmetric particles, which could explain the structure of matter and dark matter.

1018. Can Climate Change Be Reversed?—Geoengineering technologies, such as carbon sequestration, might help, but their effectiveness and consequences are uncertain.

1019. Extremophiles on Earth—Organisms thriving in extreme environments (e.g., bacteria in hydrothermal vents) suggest that life might exist in similar conditions on other planets.

1020. Colonization of Mars—Will it be possible to create a habitable environment on Mars? This question spans biology, technology, and geology.

1021. Can Consciousness Be Copied?—Transferring human consciousness to machines or cloud data remains one of the most futuristic and controversial ideas.

1022. AI Superintelligence—What will be the consequences of creating artificial intelligence that surpasses human intelligence? Can it be controlled?

1023. Unknown Forms of Life—Could life exist in forms not based on carbon and water, such as in methane or ammonia?

1024. Is Space Infinite?—If the universe is infinite, what are its structure and ultimate boundaries?

1025. New States of Matter—Discoveries of exotic states of matter, such as Bose-Einstein condensates, point to the possibility of additional unknown forms.

1026. Limits of Newtonian Physics—Newtonian physics fails at quantum and cosmic scales; what other limitations will science uncover?

1027. The Mystery of Life in the Universe—Does life arise wherever suitable conditions exist, or is it the result of an extremely rare coincidence?

1028. What Is Reality?—A fundamental question in philosophy and science: Is our reality genuine, or could it be a simulation or hologram?

An Ode to Curiosity and the Power of Science

This book is a journey through the fascinating world of science, showcasing its most groundbreaking discoveries, lingering mysteries, and bold future possibilities. From the depths of quantum mechanics to the farthest reaches of space, from the origins of life to the complex intricacies of the human brain, each chapter explores the endless curiosity that drives humanity forward. The stories of evolution, our connection to the universe, and the cutting-edge advances in technology and biology reveal the astonishing depth and breadth of our quest for knowledge. This collection celebrates the power of science to transform our understanding of reality and inspires us to keep asking the biggest questions.

Thank you for embarking on this intellectual adventure. This book would not have been possible without the support and inspiration from countless scientists, educators, and curious minds throughout history. Special gratitude goes to readers like you, who keep the flame of curiosity alive and continue to fuel the pursuit of knowledge. Your enthusiasm for learning drives the progress of science and discovery.

Your thoughts and insights mean a lot to me as an author. If this book sparked your interest, answered questions, or inspired new ones, I'd love to hear your feedback. Did any section particularly resonate with you? Are there areas where you'd like to dive deeper? Please share your reflections and suggestions—they are invaluable for future endeavors and for improving the way science is shared and celebrated. Thank you!

www.ingramcontent.com/pod-product-compliance
Lightning Source LLC
LaVergne TN
LVHW012125070526
838202LV00056B/5854